FISHERMEN'S KNITS FROM THE COAST OF NORWAY

LINE IVERSEN AND
MARGARETH SANDVIK

FISHERMEN'S KNITS FROM THE COAST OF NORWAY

A History of a Life at Sea and Over 20 New Designs Inspired by Traditional Scandinavian Patterns

Trafalgar Square
North Pomfret, Vermont

First published in the United States of America
in 2022 by
Trafalgar Square Books
North Pomfret, Vermont

Originally published in Norwegian as *Rett i Garnet: Historien om fiskerens ullklær med nye strikkeoppskrifter.*

The instructions and material lists in this book were carefully reviewed by the author and editor; however, accuracy cannot be guaranteed. The author and publisher cannot be held liable for errors.

ISBN: 978-1-64601-165-0
Library of Congress Control Number: 2022936923

Interior graphic design Type-it AS
Cover design RM Didier
Photo editor Line Iversen
Photography Marius Beck Dahle and Kristin Støylen
Publisher's editor Laila.andreassen@museumsforlaget.no
Translation into English Carol Huebscher Rhoades

Printed in China
10 9 8 7 6 5 4 3 2 1

TABLE OF CONTENTS

Preface 7
Sources 9
There's a Large Pantry, But Just as Large a Cemetery 11
The Sources Reveal: Clothing and Equipment for Surviving as a Fisherman 19
Elements of the Garments, from Innermost to Outermost 33
Producing the Garments—A Family's Work 47

Knitting Patterns

Reconstruction vs. Inspiration 62
Viking Bank 67
Frøya Bank 73
Sklinna Bank 79
Halten Bank 83
Shetland Banks 89
Træna Bank 93
West-Tampen 99
Storegga 105
Vesterål Banks 111
North Cape Bank 115
Rockall 121
Tromsø Flow 127
Spitsbergen Bank 133
Dogger Bank 139
Røst Bank 143
Fladen 147
Newfoundland Banks 153
Jyske Reef 157
Fugløy Bank 159
Utsira North 163
Orkney Islands 167
Cross Stitch Alphabet 168
Notes 170
Yarn Information 171
Sources 172

PREFACE

Humans have always needed to cover themselves with clothing, for cultural reasons or as protection against the natural elements. Along with food and shelter, clothing is one of our primary necessities; therefore, people have constantly sought cheaper and more effective ways to produce it. This book is concerned with Norwegian fishermen's clothing from the 1700s up to the 1900s, when fishermen went to sea in open boats. These fishermen were completely dependent on clothing to protect the body from weather and wind, from the innermost to the outermost garments. We'll discuss the materials, production, and use of this clothing, with particular emphasis on knitted wool garments. What did these clothes consist of? Were they conservative, or were there trends that followed fashion and economics? Who were the makers, and who were the users? Be inspired—perhaps you'll find some garments you'd like to knit.

This book is divided into two parts; the first part delves into the history behind traditional fishermen's knits, and the second contains knitting patterns and instructions for designs based on the garments Norwegian fishermen wore. We would like to continue a tradition of knitting garments especially suited for fishermen, so our patterns are adapted to today's needs for protection against weather and wind—we haven't reproduced the old garments that we describe, but rather have used them as inspiration. In relating the history behind the garments, we hope readers will reflect on the love and care that went into these pieces. There's a beautiful symbiosis between the women who worked to make warm clothing that would keep their men alive at sea, and the men who fished to keep their families alive with food.

All the patterns in this book are named for fishing banks on the Norwegian coast. Like other rock formations, each fishing bank lying under our waters has its own name, even if we can't see them with the naked eye. These banks are hidden, and today represent little-used knowledge, but by naming the garments in this book after them, we hope to commemorate the meaning they once had for fishermen and the local environment. Thank you to Erik Bolstad, head editor for *Store norske leksikon* [The Big Norwegian Encyclopedia], for his detailed overview of Norwegian fishing banks. We recommend a deep dive into the full list: https://www.erikbolstad.no/geo/noreg/fiskebankar.

The patterns in this book come in four sizes, and can be worn by either women or men. We hope that both old and young, men and women, will want to wear these garments inspired by our fishing traditions. At the same time, we encourage readers to build on these traditions and play with the patterns by substituting colors, combining different pattern panels in new ways, and paying attention to their own imaginations and powers of creativity.

Every successful adventure takes some help along the way—including this one. A big thank you to the models who lined up for us on the bank boat Storeggen of Aalesund one lovely June day in Hjørundfjorden: Egil Skarbø, Lars Leine, Theodor Iversen, Aurora Iversen, Felix Iversen, and the ship's dog, Attila Iversen. Photographer Marius Beck Dahle took the photos on the Storeggen.

In a busy rush, we had great assistants with our knitting, too. Many, many thanks to Tove Bjørkavåg, Ragnhild Flem, Inger Elisabeth Haugerud, Anne-Katrine Lindmann, Ferruh Øzalp, and Berit Krogstad.

Thanks also to the yarn companies Hillesvåg Ullvarefabrikk, Rauma Ullvarefabrikk, and Sandnes Garn, for many of the yarns for *Fishermen's Knits from the Coast of Norway*.

Greetings from
Line Iversen and Margareth Sandvik
Ålesund

SOURCES

In the work for this book, we used primary sources, secondary sources, and literature written by enterprising women with comprehensive knowledge of their subject. Many of our primary sources were items from the textile collection at the Sunnmøre Museum. By researching garments and equipment, we gained first-hand knowledge of the items and their construction. Other important primary sources included informants who had worn fishermen's garments, or who had seen how they were worn. These primary sources were supported by secondary sources such as contemporary narratives from the eighteenth to twentieth centuries, written by local officials. We would also have liked to have had contemporary sources written by the women who knitted these clothes, but the only sources we have from them are the garments they so carefully made so long ago. Texts about the fishing population were written by men with higher education, not by farmers and fishermen. We dream about diaries and accounts written by the fishermen's wives themselves, about the lives they lived and the thoughts they had, but they weren't in a position to produce such works—and we are wholeheartedly thankful for the valuable traces they did leave us, in their handwork. What we do have are sources discussing the lives of Norwegians who lived along the coast, taken down in official accounts or written by poet-priests and researchers. These sources are nothing to sneeze at, but the fact is that we can only look back on these traditional fishing communities through the eyes of local officials, educated men who had completely different resources and qualifications than the people whose lives they described. The priest, researcher, and topographer Hans Strøm (1726-1797) was an important contemporary source for information on fishermen's outfits and fisheries, along with the theologian and sociologist Eilert Sundt (1817-1875) for life in the villages. Other important secondary sources are costume watercolors, drawings, paintings, and photographs. Watercolors and drawings are important source materials for studying folk costumes from the past, and when photography became common in the 1850s, photographic costume series became an extension of these.

The ethnologist Gunvor Ingstad Trætteberg (1897-1975) was a leader in Norwegian folklife research, and one of the subjects she most certainly researched was fishermen's work clothing. She wrote two drafts of a book on sea-clothing and leather outfits in 1960 and 1966, but these books were not published until almost thirty years later, after her death. Trætteberg collected invaluable knowledge about handwork, and conducted field surveys around the country with informants who are now gone. The material she left behind is the kind we can no longer find first-hand, due to the amount of time that has passed. Her work was a natural source for us to use for our book, and is recommended for anyone interested in reading more about fishermen's leather outfits. Another important woman whose work has served as a resource for us is Ellen Kjellmo (born in 1931). She researched and wrote about the use and production of boat rya rugs (*båtrya*), and she also has a deep knowledge of native Scandinavian sheep, Spelsau sheep in particular.

THERE'S A LARGE PANTRY, BUT JUST AS LARGE A CEMETERY

"There's a large pantry, but just as large a cemetery," goes the saying in Troms, on the topic of Lofoten cod fishing.[1] This citation is applicable to all the communities that made their living from fishing along Norway's very long coastline. Take a little time to dwell on these words, and think about what they imply. Fishing could be an adventure, a source of both secure income and food, but it brought with it a gripping anxiety that anyone could be lost at sea. From the 1700s to 1900s, fishermen went out to fish in open boats, and their work meant an existence of grueling toil in rain, cold, and snow, navigating restless waves and breakwaters in tearing and icy wind. Fishermen's wives sat at home with their children and waited for their husbands, who must come back. Dying in the ice-cold water was gruesome but common, and, because it was a part of life, was also tied to folk beliefs. If you met a *draugen,* a ghost on the sea, it was undoubtedly a warning about death. Every fishing trip was a necessary risk—it was hard work, and any given fisherman might not return, but good weather and fine fishing could also allow the men to travel home with a big catch, life and limb intact. It was a double-edged sword, and a young man once told his father that he was a happy and free man when they fished so much that they paid off their banking debts. The complex relationship between fishing communities and the sea made it vital for fishermen to have clothing and equipment that both protected the body and was functional enough that they could engage in active labor. It wasn't possible to do the necessary work without such equipment, and women, especially fishermen's wives, were responsible for providing it. Fishermen's outfits consisted of many components, and the use of fishermen's clothing was similar all along the coast of Norway. However, the materials used and the traditions that informed clothing design varied from place to place.

Fishing-Farming Economy

Fiskebonde ("fisher-farmer") is a Norwegian term for a person who, as the translation implies, was both a fisherman and a farmer. In the 1700s and 1800s, there were many Norwegians who lived off both the land and sea, and it was the same all along the coast from Rogaland, at the southern end of Norway's western coast, to Finnmark in the far north, even if farming contributed significantly less than fishing up in Finnmark. Similar economies or combinations of economies were common in all of Europe. Fisher-farmers had a little arable land, a homestead, or lived as beach dwellers at the edge of the sea. There were many who didn't own their homes or the land itself, but rented from a larger landowner. A fisher-farmer rowed out to fish at the same time that he and his family worked a portion of land and kept some animals. He was completely dependent on a woman to run the home when he was out at sea with their sons, and she rightly became "the real farmer," as she was called in practice, because it was she who, for the most part, did that work, while taking care of younger children. However, the fisher-farmer men did the heaviest chores, such as mowing and haymaking, while they were ashore. Even very young children were expected to help out, and had age-appropriate roles; the girls followed their mother at work, while the boys followed their father. That way, they learned everything they would need to know when they became adults, married, and had to support their own families the same way their parents had.

To be a fisher-farmer meant always prioritizing the work that produced the highest income—for example, cod fishing and haymaking. Through the centuries, fishermen along the coast were dependent on large fishing expeditions following cod and herring, usually far from home. Cod fishing occurred in February and March, at the same time as winter herring fishing after large herring and spring herring. In the summer, fishermen want after fat herring and small herring. Then, as

Table II, figs. 1-3, from Hans Strøm, *Beskrivelse over Søndmør* [Description of Sunnmøre], 1762. Figure 1 shows a *jekt* (a small cargo boat with half deck and sails), figure 2 an *åttring*, and figure 3 a *fjørefar*. Photo: Sunnmøre Museum.

now, fishermen had to sail to wherever the fish were, and that meant that they had to travel anywhere from a couple of days to several weeks in open boats to reach the fishing grounds. The actual fishing also lasted for several weeks, and by the time that was finished, the fisher-farmer had been away from home for two to three months.[2]

Out Fishing

In 1762, Hans Strøm wrote about the various types of boats used for fishing. The boats were called *sexring, ottring, tendring, fiøringfar, færing,* and *kiempe-færing. Sexring, ottring,* and *tendring* are terms with their origins in old Norwegian names, rooted in the verb "to row." These older names describe how many oars each type of boat had; a *seksring* (*sexring*) had six oars, an *åttring* (*ottring*) had eight oars, and a *tiroing* (*tendring*) had ten oars. Strøm wrote that the *åttring* is a name that dates all the way back to 1240, where it was used in Hagen Hagensøn's history in Snorre Sturlason's chronicles, but he could not confirm that it meant the same type of boat as the term *åttring* when used in the eighteenth century, as shown in Table II (fig 2).[3] Strøm wrote the following in 1788 about the spring fishing in Sunnmøre:

> For the Fishing Expedition, one needed a complete Boat with Sails and Rigging, a so-called *Fjørefar* (or *Fiæringfar*) with four pairs of Oars manned by six men [...] It has been stated that there were 500 such Boats costing a total of 20,291 riksdaler[4] and 4 marks[5]. Such a boat can well be used for 10 Years or even 12 Years.[6]

Strøm's estimate here—that fishing required a good seafaring boat, a *fjørefar*, crewed by six men, and that there were 500 such boats employed during this expedition in Sunnmøre—means that 3,000 men were out on the spring fishing in the 1780s, all of whom would have needed clothing and equipment.

An *åttring* was a common boat used for fishing in the nineteenth century, usually with a crew of seven men. Up until 1840, it was common for two to four fisher-farmers to jointly own an *åttring*, although by 1850-1860, increasing numbers had bought their boat on their own. They depended on traveling oarsmen to man the boats. The author Arnold Farstad (born in 1948) has in-depth knowledge of fisheries. He wrote that the fishing fleet in Haram doubled from 1840 to 1860, from about 50 *åttring* boats to 100, and that there weren't enough local men to handle that amount of cod fishing. This also meant that there were even more men who needed clothing and equipment. An oarsmen's contract from Vikebukt in Romsdalen relates details about two young men, Lars and John, who went to sea on the Sjur-ottringen from Løvsøya on Sunnmøre in 1878:

> The undersigned Lars Ottesen Vige and John Kundsen Vige acknowledge today that we have agreed to attach ourselves as oarsmen to Marthinus Rasmussen Lausund for this year's cod fishing, for pay of 15 speciedaler for the journey and free meals, as well as committing ourselves to defend our space on the boat as commonly capable people. Aalesund 2 February 1878.[7]

Lars was 25 years old and came from a homestead, and John was 19 and came from a more prosperous farm. The pay they received was the same: 60 crowns and free food. Oarsmen had set pay, and for the most part, the amount was completely independent of how long it took to reach the fishing they were contracted to. In addition, an oarsman's pay could vary from year to year. The amount of the catch, fish prices during previous seasons, and how skilled one was as an oarsman also played a role. Normally, large farmers, sons of small farmers, and boys could make enough to set a little money aside. But all were subject to the whims of the weather. February and March were months that often brought many storms and strong winds, and bad weather led to staying on land. An åttring was a seaworthy boat, but because it was an open boat, it clearly had its limitations. Besides the weather, fish prices and the movements of cod populations from year to year were factors that could also influence the outcome of the fishing. One example of how much the catch could vary is the average number of fish for the winter fishing for Haram and Vigra for the years 1868 to 1886.[8] These catch numbers show the amount of cod caught per participating vessel. Imagine being out on an open boat on the sea, and either dragging cod after cod on board, or sitting there with a lump in your stomach because there weren't any fish.

YEAR	NUMBER OF COD FISH PER BOAT
1868	1800
1869	2747
1870	2508
1871	1414
1872	3636
1873	2562
1874	1866
1875	2500
1876	1600
1879	1262
1880	3670
1881	2742
1882	1593
1883	746
1884	2000
1885	1091
1886	4687

At the end of the day during a season's fishing, the fishermen returned to land and took care of the day's catch before they could berth. The crew lived in shanties, *fjordmansstover* ("fishers' cottages"), or salvaged flat beds over the large boathouse floor during the time the fishing lasted. The smallest boats often did not have room for their crews to stay on board overnight, so the men needed housing on land. Fishermen in larger boats, however, could stay on the boat overnight under a canvas. The men laid the sails down as a covering over the bow and slept in a group. It wasn't uncommon for them to have to brush snow off themselves when they got up the next morning. A shanty could hold up to ten men, and had berths where two or three people slept together. These shanties weren't insulated, and often had flooring that was partly wood and partly earth. Cooking and repairs of fishing equipment and such took place on the small floor space between berths. Close living conditions meant that sickness and pests spread rapidly. It was not easy to keep clean in the shanties, and personal hygiene was bad.[9] In the north of the country, it was common for boys to go out on the Lofoten cod fishing as cook's boys when they were 12-14 years old. Then

A *trerøring*, also called a *snidbetning*—a "sloped boat"—had three pairs of oars and was a suitable boat for coastal fishing, as a church boat, a shuttle boat, and for cattle freight. This boat is now housed in the Sunnmøre Museum and was likely built around 1860 for a fishing group in Rovde in Vanylven. Photo: Line Iversen.

they had the task of preparing food and trying to keep the shanties in order. Otherwise, the children had to row out for fish to boil and coastal fishing was an important supplement for both people and animals. It meant fresh food for the family and quick feed in the barn. Pieces cut off of either squid or herring were good dinners for the animals.[10]

Home on the Farm

At home on the farm, it was the women who had all the responsibility and care of the house, animals and land. One of the county governors of Sunnmøre related that in his district, an average farm had 1 horse, 10 large cattle, 30 small cattle, and 1 pig, and usually raised about 30 barrels of grain and 20 barrels of potatoes.[11]

Working days were long, and the concepts of free time and vacations didn't exist. Due to the clear divisions between gender roles and the large amount of work, it was necessary to have both men and women on the farm, and usually it was a married couple. To keep the farm going, it was also common to marry again very quickly after a spouse died. If a man had to support a family, he needed an income, and it could take a long time before a farm was available so that younger people could marry and take over the work. People

This *fjordmannsstova* was built in Fosnavåg, on the archipelago of Herøy, in 1868 and today is part of the Sunnmøre Museum. The islanders called such shanties *fjordmansstover* after the people who owned them. The owners themselves called them "fishers' cottages" or "barracks." This cottage has room for two boat groups, with space for beds for up to fourteen men and a cook. Photo: Kristin Støylen.

might get up into their thirties before getting the chance to marry; in the meantime, they worked as hired farm hands or servant girls. The burden of work on a married couple was great, and the gendered division of labor was such that a man would not do "women's work," but a woman could and would step in for a man to take on any work task. Of course, there were exceptions. Women were responsible for the planning and execution of all food preparation, as well as making, repairing, and washing clothes. This included hard work and elaborate processes. In indigenous Sami communities, however, it was not uncommon for men to cook. Women were also responsible for the care of livestock, and for growing food for people and animals, in addition to tending to all of the members of the household—not least, their own children. Women also cared for a farm's pensioners and paupers. All of this was done with a minimum of aids. Today, we can scarcely imagine the working conditions these women lived with, given such a large amount of work and so much wear and tear. The same, of course, also applied to men. Crop failures and poor fishing directly affected every household's ability to have sufficient means to support itself; you can just imagine the concerns these women had over whether any given year would yield enough to feed their families. Given all this, we can understand that a wife's anxiety about the fisher-farmer away at sea revolved around not only love, but the survival of her and hers.

Higher-class officials had little understanding of the conditions the fisherman and his family lived under. They had difficulty recognizing that these fishing communities didn't enjoy the same living standards they had, not to mention they didn't have the same resources, either. The county governor wrote that even if these "common people" had increased economic well-being, it wouldn't have improved their unsanitary way of life. Lack of cleanliness and bad hygiene were prominent in most districts and especially in coastal districts.[12]

This problem with hygiene was recorded in several reports, and showed a clear difference between fishing communities and "enlightened" upper society. Having a little money wasn't the same as having "class." Eilert Sundt was also frustrated by the coastal population's living standards. In 1873, his writings about traveling around Sunnmøre, visiting and talking with people, were like a "historic study." He found this very interesting, and wrote that "the language was quite old-fashioned, as was conduct and their mode of living also." The area was very traditional and simple, even if it was considered the "shabby Vestland." The state of the houses and the style of cooking were scarcely satisfactory, in his view. The floors were scrubbed on every second or third Saturday, tables and benches every Saturday, and the washing up was never sufficient. Sundt did find happy exceptions that suited him—for example, in the islands of Herøy, where people washed the windows, tables, benches, and floors two times a week. He was also disappointed in personal hygiene; people didn't wash their faces and hands daily, no matter what work they'd done that day. Washing was also often limited to faces and hands. Many people didn't wash their bodies or hair, though they did comb their hair perhaps once a week, or if going out to travel or for some special reason. The exception was again on Herøy, where the residents washed their hands after working with fish and the "hands and also the head were washed." It was incomprehensible to Sundt that people could be so dirty, and he wrote:

> However much one writes about shabbiness on account of poverty, *water is a cheap item* and here so easily available, that it is neither a sacrifice of time nor money to rinse the snuff off before going in to eat [...].[13]

Young people were better at keeping themselves clean by bathing in the sea, among other methods. Impurity was only increased by the fact that most people changed their clothes every fourteenth day, and even then, sometimes it was only their undergarments. Sundt wished that people would open their eyes to the economic gains to be made by washing themselves and changing their clothes more often, because then their clothes would last longer. He thought all this came from people's way of thinking, and not because they simply didn't have the means to bathe regularly or keep an extra change of clothes they weren't using. When it came to the cleanliness of the houses, Sundt thought it was a matter of the construction of the house, with the kitchen, work space, and bedrooms all in one—it was impossible to have "urban cleanliness" under such conditions, and one couldn't just tell people to build an extra room. Men's use of tobacco, which they spit out on the floor, made them responsible for the poor housekeeping—together with the building customs. Dirty pots and cups were the fault of women.[14]

Upper-class men didn't only have problems with the

fisher-farmers' hygiene and housekeeping, but also considered the condition of their farms in general reprehensible. Fishing and farming were, in fact, done exactly as they had been for generations. Fisher-farmers didn't like change, even if it meant economic gains if they would just follow the advice of the authorities. The authorities would have preferred economic growth in their districts, and even showed how it could be done. Official records from the 1850s were, in some sections, dramatic reading when it came to farming. The same reports mention that people could experience poor fishing, which caused material prosperity to decline temporarily, while fishermen could gain surprisingly large dividends based on the rising prices. This money was used for official contributions and payments, as well as improvement of people's way of life and clothing.[15]

But at the same time, it was common all around Norway for farmers to keep as many sheep and cows as possible, more than they could support, and starve them over the winter. The animals that didn't die of starvation were then released onto the spring pastures, and ate down what would become the hay harvest for the fall, reducing yield. The fisher-farmer wasn't interested in hearing that these methods resulted in less and less production, and created a negative spiral; it was simply how things had always been done. Even a valuable horse could starve over the winter. The stall and barn were small, dark, and close, which worsened bad conditions for the animals. Manure was stored in such a way that water ran through it, which removed all the nutrients. This also went against the clear recommendations of the authorities, which came up again and again in official reports.

Local officials wanted farmers to retire old fields and meadows, and break up new fields where the soil wasn't so exhausted. That would provide good, plentiful winter feed for their cows, which would produce more milk, of better quality. The cows would then also produce more and better manure, which would soon improve the fields. But farmers had trouble following these methods. Newly-cleared fields, meant to replace old ones, wouldn't yield the same returns for the first few years. In the meantime, the farmer was forced to buy grain, which was perceived as a significant loss. Farmers were also very skeptical about shifting to newer, more expensive farming equipment; they preferred to keep to simple wooden tools, to the great frustration of the authorities. That was a common tendency for farmers and householders all around Norway. The county governor reported that farming had stalled at "the low stage," in short supply of insight and capital throughout the nineteenth century. But, he reflected, this was a given, since much of the arable land in Norway had been used by builders and tenants who, naturally, were not interested in working toward the lasting improvement of land they did not themselves own.[16] The same applied to houses on these farms. Tenant farmers didn't want to invest in windows, painting, or upgrading buildings that sooner or later would be abandoned when they could no longer work. They couldn't take upgrades like these with them when they could no longer pay their rent and ended up on poor relief. It wasn't until the 1890s that people began to open up to the advantages of modern farming methods and were willing to change their ways of thinking.

These were the conditions the authorities thought the fisher-farmers and their families lived under—a long way from their own reality and standards. These criticisms were well intended, but perhaps those who made them had too little understanding of the amount of work these people had for improving the management of their farms and homes. Were fishing communities really so backwards and stubborn? Not in all respects. We will soon see that both women and men had unique knowledge, including in regards to producing fishermen's clothing. This knowledge came from generations of experience—and partly from conservatism. They'd found a formula that worked, and it wasn't something to be changed for just any reason. Despite their alleged lack of understanding of hygiene and household management, these families worked hard for each other. Their uncertainty about potential crop and fishing failures drove their work forward—they couldn't take time off or neglect going out to fish. And in order to go to sea, the fisherman-farmer was totally dependent on help from his wife.

THE SOURCES REVEAL: CLOTHING AND EQUIPMENT FOR SURVIVING AS A FISHERMAN

Written Sources

Much as for farming, fishing equipment and boats changed very slowly over time. This equipment consisted of what was needed to survive and perform hard labor both on the open sea, and when fishing along the coast and in the fjords. Survival revolved around warming the body and keeping hunger away from the stomach. On a season's fishing trip, the fisherman had to take everything he needed with him: food, clothing, and bedding to last for the duration of the journey—though, of course, they had a ready supply of fresh fish along the way. Various sources relate that leather outer clothing and wool inner- and under-garments were common all around the country for fishing in open boats. In addition, men took bedding in the form of sheepskins or handwoven coverings, rya coverlets, and pillows.

The Norwegian word *hyre* signifies the outer garments fishermen and seafarers wore when they worked at sea. Language researcher and poet Ivar Aasen (1813-1896) wrote that the verb *hyre* meant "to supply or equip oneself," particularly with clothing. When the word *hyre* refers to a complete outfit, it means "equipment." The concept of leather outfits encompasses all the leather garments used for fishing, but not the clothing worn under them. In Troms, South Trøndelag, Hordaland, and North Hordaland, people also used the word *våsklede* instead of *hyre*. According to Aasen, this word signifies difficult travel in bad weather and storms. We can also find the term in Norwegian and Icelandic tales and on deeds from the Middle Ages. Leather equipment was smooth, indicating that the hair had been removed.[17]

Since fishing was an important part of life and the economy along the coast, there are numerous secondary sources about this work. Hans Strøm described the standard fisherman's outfit in detail in 1762, with the accompanying drawing in *Table IV*.

Strøm tells us that the farmers' clothing was quite similar overall, but there were differences between those who lived on the coast and islands, and those who lived along the fjords. One of those differences is the *vadmal* garments called "wool shirts," which were short out on the islands and only went down just below the belt, but were longer and longer the further you went into the fjords. The longest reached below the knees, and hid both the vest and other undershirts, which were shorter and worn underneath. Strøm inferred from this that farmers who also fished often were more comfortable working in wool shirts that were shorter. Fisher-farmers had several other garments that suited their work specifically, such as sailcloth trousers (called canvas), and leather treated with cod-liver oil. Fisher-farmers also wore leather hats, similar to regular hats in shape except that they didn't fold up, lined with *vadmal*. For outer garments, fishermen wore leather sleeves, or short sleeves made of leather and a *skinnstakk*, a "leather

Table IV, figures 1-5, from Hans Strøm's *Beskrivelse over Søndmør* [Description of Sunnmøre], 1762. Photo: Sunnmøre Museum.

skirt"—a wide jacket, made of the same material as for the leather hat and leather trousers, with a small opening at the chest so it could be pulled on over the head. These leather skirts were only worn at sea, writes Strøm; for everyday wear, the fisher-farmer wore a *bringeskinn*, which was a piece of leather which hung from the neck down onto the chest and was attached around the waist, like a leather apron. Men wore boots most of the time, except in the fjord areas, where men were primarily engaged in farming and wore *snøsokker*, a kind of spats or legging. Figure 3 in Table IV shows the fishermen's costume, while figure 1 clearly shows the *bringeskinn* over a sweater, with an opening all the way down the front. Strøm wrote that the fjord farmers wore suede leather pants instead of sailcloth pants or leather imbued with cod-liver oil. They also wore lined caps instead of leather hats. Fjord farmers had buttons on their sweaters and buckles on their shoes, while fisher-farmers used clasps and shoe straps. Finally, Strøm found it strange that even though the fjords were bitterly cold, people there wore lighter clothing than those living on the coast. They wore only a long jacket and vest without a scarf, while islanders wore two or three jackets or sweaters, as well as a breast cloth and scarf.

Strøm offered a detailed—to a fault—written source about fishermen's manner of dress, and did his own drawings to illustrate what he wrote. In the book he published 26 years after Description of *Sunnmøre*, he also wrote about leather outfits:

> On such a Fjørefar or large Sea Boat, there are always six Men who must be supplied with Leather clothing, consisting of Boots, large Leather Jackets or a so-called Leather Skirt, as well as Leather Trousers [...].[18]

Sea garments clearly still followed the same traditions as ever. The leather jacket was an outer garment, as was the leather skirt, but with the front opening buttoned. The leather skirt as described here has nothing to do with women's skirts; the term "leather skirt" became used for this closed leather jacket along the entire coast. In most places, both the leather skirt and leather jacket were worn in the same villages. Leather pants were called *brok* or *bukse*.

On Sunnmøre and in Hordaland, the fishermen's leather pants were also called *va-brok* or *va-bukse*. Hans Strøm wrote in 1762 that the word *va* referred to a fishing rope. *Va-brok* were, therefore, the pants men wore when pulling in ropes, and the most important garment in the sea outfit. Ivar Aasen has the same interpretation.[19]

The poet-priest Petter Dass (1647-1707) wrote about the equipment for Lofoten cod fishing in *Nordland's Trumpet* (published posthumously in 1739):

> We made 3 months of food for our boys,
> 12 Bismerpund[20] of butter and 12 Bismerpund of cheese,
> Flatbread of proper weight;
> Indeed barley for soup, Meat, and of Stompbread a pound,
> Indeed an Iron stone and Leather skirt with boots so round
> Indeed resplendent with bait hooks and fish hooks.
> But then not even satisfying their wants,
> A cask of buttermilk[21] we made for them.
> And so their food casks crammed full;
> Yes, that I will in short report,
> We provisioned them until the pantry was empty,
> So we scarcely had enough for our meals.[22]

Dass described the food and drink young men took with them, and informed us that it went beyond the stores left for those who remained on the farm. He also related that they had leather skirts and boots. A century later, in 1834, the theologian and parish priest Iver Ancher Heltzen (1785-1842) mentioned some of the same equipment:

> A man going to the Lofoten cod fishing had to be equipped with a single good Food chest, about which we'll speak immediately, but also good Leather clothes, hereby understood as a Leather skirt, which was a Jacket made of skin, almost of the same shape, as described above; a pair of Leather Trousers, these were short, and very wide, cut off at the Knees; a pair of Sea boots which had to be good quality and completely watertight, they came up to the thighs, so they could go up under the trousers described here; a Leather Hat and a Pair of Sea Mittens. This is the outfit that protected the Body during the Winter cold and under this our People from Rana wore a Breast cloth, 2 Vests, a Sweater, but generally only a Leather sweater lined with sheepskin. The head was only provided with a red Cap, under the Leather hat, just as in the Summer, when the sun shines with the most burning Heat.[23]

Heltzen wrote that a fisherman must have a leather skirt, leather trousers, sea boots that go up to the thigh, a leather hat, and sea mittens. Under the sea outfit, the fisherman would wear a breast cloth, vest, sweater, and leather jacket with wool, plus a red cap. The red cap was also worn in the summer, no matter how much the sun fried one's head. Heltzen continued, listing the food provisions:

> The Food Items which a Master was obligated to give to his Servants traveling to the Lofoten cod fishing were as follows: 50.69 lb / 23.04 kg Flatbread; 22.6 lb / 10.28kg Stompbread or Rye bread; 22.6 lb / 10.28 kg Barley flour for soup; 11.3 lb / 5.14 kg old Cheese; 11.3 lb / 5.14 kg Butter; 1 whole Body of a smoked Sheep or Goat; 1 Barrel Buttermilk, some salted Meat; 2 Milk Cheeses, 20 Lefse and 2.2 oz / 62.5 g herring. In addition, 1 to 2 Jugs Schnapps as well as a few ounces of tobacco. It goes without saying that many traveled with fewer supplies, or supplied themselves for fishing, when they were poor, but there was scarcely a hired man or fisherman who was supplied by a wealthy man, who supplied the traveler with a smaller food chest. When now finally everything was stored in the chest and barrels, the Servant was readied by his Master and could receive the Fishing Equipment which he would use during the fishing expedition.[24]

In 1863, Eilert Sundt offered this description of the leather outfit in Tromsø by O. C. Berge:

> As promised, I am sending a report on the local fishermen's outfit. Outer clothing "Hyre," Sea socks, Leather Trousers, Leather Skirt, Sou'wester or Felt Hat, Sea Boots, Leather Strips for arm wraps, Mittens.[25]

Berge calculated the weight of the leather clothes and found out that they weighed 31.5 marks altogether, or about 17.25 pounds / 7.8 kilos. He reminds us that leather clothes and mittens increase in weight when they are wet.

Trætteberg interviewed an informant in 1958 who had first-hand knowledge of what it was like to travel for a season's fishing in an open boat. Edvin Kampevoll (born in 1882) from Tranøybotn, on Senja, was 76 years old when he told her the following about bedding and food:

> A thick rug (*grene*)[26] for the bottom blanket and a similar one for the top blanket. It was all stuck inside a sackcloth. Or one used a sheepskin. In later years, we had to cover up with the sheepskin and some used reindeer skin for the bottom layer. We each wove our own rugs. We had a head pillow with a handwoven half-wool cover. It was striped in red or other colors. The pillow was filled with rags and reindeer hair. We took off our leather clothes at night. As a general rule, our journey clothing was kept separate and not stored together with the clothing we wore on land. In the old days, before we had shelter on the boat, we had our clothes in a barrel in the forward. We kept our food in a chest and a large pot we could heat. We boiled coffee in a pot. We had kegs of sour milk. We had provisions for two months. A barrel of flatbread was baked. The pieces were put four together when it was done. It was laid under a press so it wouldn't take up too much room. Four to six kilos (8.8 to 13.2 pounds) of butter was enough. That was all a man had. Cured meats and a couple of shoulders (from a sheep) were good or what one now had. Other breads we had included a chest of *klappcake* baked on a large round iron slab (a griddle), or thin cake baked in an oven. Those were made with water and coarse rye flour. They were about 6-8 in / 15-20 cm in diameter. They were thicker than pancakes. When we finished the fishing, we bought a homecoming drink and a string of Bergen pretzels. Otherwise, while fishing, we had mashed liver and fresh fish and roe. We laid fish on the flatbread. We were often two to a boat team, but we each cooked in our own pot. Each team was 4-6, eventually up to 7 men with line or nets. Each man had his own nets.[27]

Kristine Lind Grøttland (1883-1973) was a teacher and administrator in Gratangen, and wrote the following overview about the clothing for Lofoten cod fishing for adult men and cook's boys in the 1890s:

Adult Men:

5-6 wool shirts (5-6 changes)
5-6 underpants (5-6 changes)
3 wool nightshirts
5 pairs of stockings
2 pairs of large sea boot socks
2 pairs of small sea boot socks
1 leather hat
Necktie (*cravat*)
Common vest
1 hunting vest
1 set of good *vadmal* clothing
1 outer jacket
2 pairs of everyday *vadmal* pants, one lined with leather in back and on the knees.
5 pairs white sea mittens
1 pair work mittens
1 work blouse (*pusseronk*)[28] to wear when sitting in the berth repairing nets or line.
Sunday outfit including a shirt
Sea boots and *røyserter* (knee-high boots with lower back)

Cook's Boys:

4 new white wool shirts (a change of clothes was a shirt and pants)
2 new wool dyed nightshirts
4 new white under-pants
2 new handwoven and handsewn outer trousers
1 thick good jacket with vest
1 thick good outer jacket
1 leather hat
1 necktie (*cravat*)
4 pairs long stockings
2 pairs small sea boot socks
2 pairs sea mittens
1 overshirt for wearing on Sunday
Sunday outfit
Leather heavy over-slippers (*lugger*) to wear in the berth
Wooden clogs, shoes, and *røyserter* (knee-high boots with lower back)[29]

Grøttland wrote nothing about wearing the leather outfit at the end of the nineteenth century, but notes that they wore vadmal clothing instead. As far as bedding, she related that the fishermen had bolsters covered by handwoven canvas or burlap and a handwoven pillow for the head. The bottom layer was a thick rug or four calf skins sewn together to a calfskin pelt. They also had burlap towels to dry their hands on.[30]

Reports also note that the men had some of the same foods on the Lofoten cod fishing from the seventeenth and into the twentieth centuries. The same also goes for bedding and clothing.

Boat Ryas—a Copy of Spelsau Wool Fleeces

Old sources also discuss the use of boat ryas (*båtryer*) used on the fishing journeys, not to mention that there are numerous examples of them in museums and in private ownership. Ivar Ancher Heltzen wrote in 1834 that one used "woven rugs with wool pile that are called 'Ryer' as bedding out on the islands on the Helgeland coast."[31] Eilert Sundt made the same observation in 1869. At the Sunnmøre Museum, we are lucky to have more than forty boat ryas. In this region, they are also called *napparyer* after the way they are made—with short strands knotted into the weaving. Boat ryas were used as bedding by low-income people, servants, fishermen out on the fishing boat, and in fishermen's shanties. Otherwise, sheepskins were common bedding up to the twentieth century, but they were not suitable when out for fishing. The information in this section is based on the work of Ellen Kjellmo, as well as our own research on the ryas in the collections at the Sunnmøre Museum.

A boat rya is a woven rug with a smooth front, and a floss or pile on the back. Boat ryas were made to keep fishermen warm. They would roll up in these rugs when they slept on their boats, or use it as an over- or under-layer when overnighting in a shanty. Preserved boat ryas capture a fantastic tradition in terms of their scope, execution, and use. The oldest preserved rya from Norden (a geographic and cultural area including Norway, Sweden, Finland, Denmark, Iceland, Greenland, and the Faroe Islands) dates to the seventeenth century, but ryas have likely existed since Viking times. Sunnmøre Museum has two ryas dated to before 1850, and the rest are from the second half of the nineteenth century. Boat ryas were especially numerous in coastal districts, and they were common equipment for fishermen in northern Norway. The weaving of boat ryas had mostly ended by the beginning of the twentieth century, but could have continued here and there long into the new century. This decline coincided with the switch from open boats to closed-deck boats—there simply was no longer a need for them.

The design of boat ryas is nothing short of brilliant; as you'll see, they're constructed the same way as the fleece of a Spelsau sheep! These weavings are a fantastic invention by our Norwegian foremothers, who were comprehensively familiar with the characteristics of their sheep, in and out. The undercoat of Spelsau sheep consists of crimpy, soft, airy wool that insulates, while the outer coat has long, coarse hair that repels water and wind. Boat ryas are made with a base, lightly woven in twill with tightly spun yarn made with coarse fibers. Then, short pile is densely knotted to that base, so the piles partially overlap to make a warm, insulating layer. This weaving technique means that the piles do not lie flat, side by side, but are arranged in several layers, which captures more air between individual strands. The same occurs on the floss side, creating even more small air-filled spaces between the fibers in the thick, soft yarn that is used for the pile. Of course, the wool for ryas came from Spelsau sheep in the first place, with the outer coat used for the warp thread and the undercoat for the pile. The weft was of a simpler quality, and was not beaten in particularly hard. This, combined with the spacing between the piles, made ryas very flexible—easy to wrap around the body. This technique required the highest level of weaving skill, because boat ryas are large and rather heavy. They could be up to 2.19 x 1.9 yards / 2 x 1.7 meters, and weigh a total of 13.2 to 39.6 pounds / 6 to 18 kilos. The heaviest rya at the Sunnmøre Museum weighs 22 pounds / 10 kilos.

The base of a rya is woven on three or four shafts in diagonal twill or in point twill, goose-eye, or rosepath. The pattern is symmetrical, in stripes or blocks, and the weaving technique is warp-faced. Two or three colors of warp threads form the pattern. Common colors were black, red, brown, gray, white, and green, in various combinations. Before 1850, yarn was dyed with plant material; after that date, ryas were woven with natural sheep's color, plant-dyed, or chemically-dyed yarns, all of which might be used in a single rya. Cow's hair was also commonly used and, in that case, was blended with wool for a weft yarn. Several of the boat ryas in the Sunnmøre Museum contain cow's hair; Eilert Sundt wrote that cow's hair was used to save yarn. However, cow's hair and horse tail-hair also have a quality that keeps knitted garments from becoming stiff when they are soaked in water, which leads us to believe that there were more reasons than Sundt understood to use cow's hair in boat ryas. The use of cow's hair might have been a conscious choice by women who knew what they were doing, not just a cost-saving measure. Pile was made with yarn spun especially for the purpose, or yarn left over from clothing worked in various materials. The wool quality of the pile yarn was soft but strong, and as thick as a pencil. This yarn was spun tightly so it wouldn't split with hard use. Pile yarn was used in natural sheep's wool colors, such as black, gray, white, and heathered shades that camouflaged the grime accumulated through hard use. The length of a rya's pile was determined by the distance between pile rows, and varied from 2 to 3½ inches / 5 to 9 cm. It was important for the piles to overlap well. A "pile rolling pin" was used to trim pile to the right length. This was a cylindrical tool with a slot for scissors. The yarn was wound onto the rolling pin and then cut off. Rows of pile were knotted on as the base was woven, usually with one every ⅜–¾ in / 1–2 cm. Usually the oldest child knotted the pile, using a knot called a smyrna knot. Knotting was done in an open shed, and the weaving technique used for ryas hid these knots so they weren't visible on the back side. This also protected the knots from wearing through, and made boat ryas very durable.[32]

The piles could be either blended without any attention paid to color arrangement, or knotted to create patterns such as blocks, monograms, or dates. Of the boat ryas preserved in the Sunnmøre Museum, about half have patterns or monograms, while the rest are mixed. Some of these ryas also have rya patches in black *klede* (firmly fulled wool fabric) with monograms or names worked in cross stitch, and colorful embroidery. The museum also has many boat ryas with pile worked in fibers other than wool. Here you'll find scraps of the most fantastic fabrics, everything from wool with block printing—which must have once been on an elegant garment—to the finest cotton fabrics. It was also common to have pile of heavy *vadmal*, wool fabric, linsey-woolsey, linen, embroidery, and machine- and hand-knitted pieces, all of which makes for a fantastic play of color in the ryas in the museum. Rag pile was cut into long strips or, even better, split along the center without cutting a piece off entirely, so every tiny little bit of spare fabric could be used. Incorporating pile of various materials was a way of recycling, making a little go a long way, and making use of whatever was on hand. For boat ryas intended for fishing journeys, however, it was important to have wool pile, because it was so much warmer than rag pile. Some of the ryas in the Sunnmøre Museum have mostly rag piles, and thus were probably used in the home rather than at sea. The museum also has many examples with only wool pile, as described here. Ryas with a lot of rag piles were not as valuable as those with only wool pile. Sundt wrote that buying a boat rya in 1840 cost all of 5 spesidaler,[33] while ryas with various different materials were generally worth from 1 to 3 spesidaler, depending on execution and condition. This shows that boat ryas were very important as fishermen's equipment, with qualities that other bedding lacked to keep fishermen warm at night.

Sheepskin, a common type of bedding, didn't function well for fishing in an open boat. It didn't tolerate water well, and during a fishing season, it would be exposed to a lot of moisture in the form of sea water and rain. The same problems can occur when a sheepskin is washed. In a humid environment, sheepskin rots, and the wool falls off. On the other hand, boat ryas tolerated all sorts of damp conditions, and could be washed without falling apart. That was a big advantage, because a heavily used boat rya could be dirty, would smell of sweat, fishing tackle, and cod-liver oil—and could attract pests. But that doesn't mean a boat rya was easy to keep clean. After fishing, a rya was laid in a large tub with soapy water, using homemade soap containing tallow, caustic soda, and ammonia. This mixture was commonly used in coastal villages. Women then stepped into the tubs and stomped on the rya for a good while, after which it was taken down to the shore. There, it was attached to the pier and rinsed clean when the tide came in. Afterwards, it was hung on the boathouse to dry, and then put away until the next fishing expedition.[34]

Despite the extreme conditions and great mechanical wear, boat ryas were very durable, and could be used by more than one generation. Many of the ryas in the Sunnmøre Museum have lasted a long time, and testify to their own durability. Pile may wear out, but the knots hold, and the weaving is elastic and keeps its shape. Boat ryas that were worn through could be used as floor rugs or recycled.

During the Second World War, there was a huge lack of various materials, and therefore many boat ryas were taken to wool mills to be shredded into shoddy. Shoddy is wool derived from shredded rags, and was used for comforters or mattress fill. Comforters were made with carded wool that had been stitched—sewn in—to a cotton covering.[35] Despite this recycling, many boat ryas have been preserved, and that says something about the scope of what must once have existed.

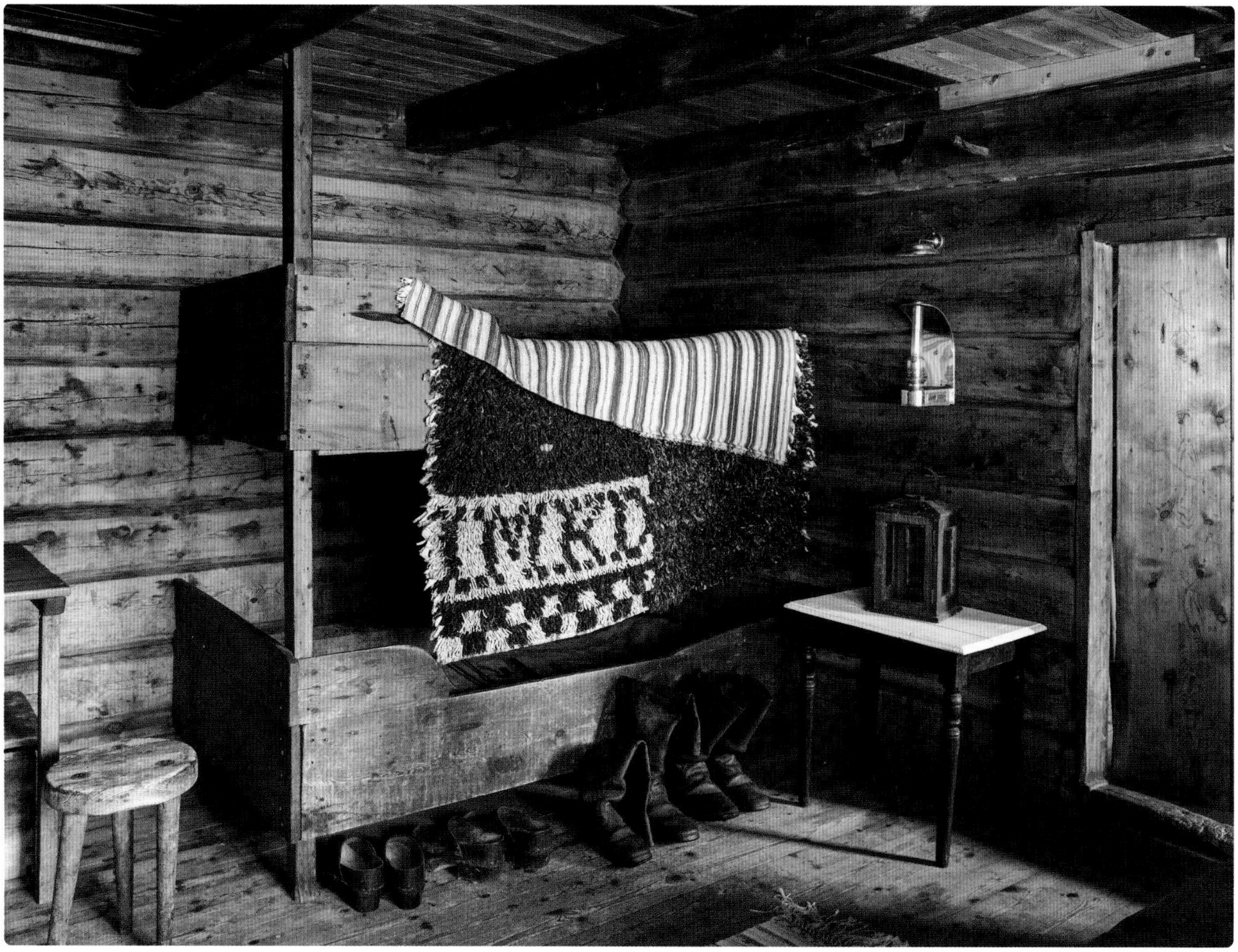

Boat rya in the Sunnmøre Museum. Photo: Kristin Støylen.

The photo above shows a boat rya or pile rya from Stranda, dating to the end of the nineteenth century. It was woven in three-shaft point twill, with two-ply wool warp thread and three-ply hemp weft. The striped pattern is worked in natural white, red, green, and violet. The width of the weaving is sewn together with hemp thread and hemmed with hemp thread on the top short side. The long sides have selvedges, and the lower short side is hemmed with hemp thread and reinforced with a row of stab stitch in red two-ply wool thread, embellished with a vine in green two-ply wool thread below. The wool pile is a combination of light-colored wool yarn and dark shoddy yarn. The edge has cotton pile, with purchased fabric in natural, white, red, brown, blue, pink, and gray. The rug has the monogram "I M K D" and a checkerboard panel.

Length: 61 in / 155 cm

Width: 58¼ in / 148 cm

Length of pile: 2 in / 5 cm

Weight: 12.3 lbs / 5.6 kg

Fishermen's Garments in the Sunnmøre Museum

In the Sunnmøre Museum collection, we have several original garments that were used by fishermen that correspond to those described in source materials. The collection contains more preserved leather than knitted garments. Because knitted garments from the period are lacking, there isn't a complete fisher-farmer's outfit at the museum. The fisherman's leather outfit is a distinct outer costume, carefully tailored for its need and sewn the same way all along the coast; by contrast, knitted undergarments and coverings for the head could vary in different districts.

UNDER-SWEATERS

UNDER-SWEATER WITH SHORT SLEEVES

Handknitted, short-sleeved under-sweater in natural white fine two-ply wool yarn. Knit two, purl two ribbing with a square neckline. The body is seamed by hand on both long sides, with the sleeves seamed on the underside and then sewn to the body.

Length: 28¼ in / 72 cm
Width: 12¼ in / 31 cm
Length of sleeve: 8 in / 20 cm
Width of neck: 7 in / 18 cm

UNDER-SWEATER WITH ¾-LENGTH SLEEVES

Handknitted sweater with ¾-length sleeves in natural white fine two-ply wool yarn. Knit one, purl one ribbing. The sleeves have knit two, purl two ribbing. A square neckline with a placket and knitted button band with two buttons covered with cotton canvas. The buttons close on the right side. The body is seamed by hand on both long sides, with the sleeves seamed on the underside and then sewn to the body. In Troms, ribbed sweaters with short or ¾-length sleeves were only worn by women.

Length: 27½ in / 70 cm
Width: 18¼ in / 46.5 cm
Length of sleeve: 13 in / 33 cm
Width of ribbing: 2½ in / 6 cm
Width of neck: 7¾ in / 19.5 cm
Length of neck placket: 5¼ in / 13 cm

UNDER-SWEATER WITH LONG SLEEVES

Handknitted, felted under-sweater with long sleeves in natural white fine two-ply wool yarn. Stockinette with lower edge in knit one, purl one ribbing. The sleeves are

Photo: Kristin Støylen.

knitted in the round with knit one, purl one ribbing. A square neckline with a placket and button band with three mother-of-pearl buttons. The buttons are sewn onto the right side. The front bands are natural-colored two-shaft woven cotton, sewn on by machine. The neckband or kvaren is edged with the same fabric as the front bands. The body is seamed by hand on the long sides, with the sleeves sewn to the body.

Length: 27½ in / 70 cm
Width: 15¾ in / 40 cm
Length of sleeve: 18¼ in / 46 cm
Width of ribbing at lower edge: 3¼ in / 8 cm
Width of ribbing on sleeves: 4½ in / 11.5 cm
Width of neck: 5½ in / 14 cm
Length of neck placket: 8¼ in / 21 cm
Width of front bands: 1½ in / 4 cm
Width of *kvare* on neckband: ⅜ in / 1 cm

WHITE MONOGRAMMED STOCKINGS

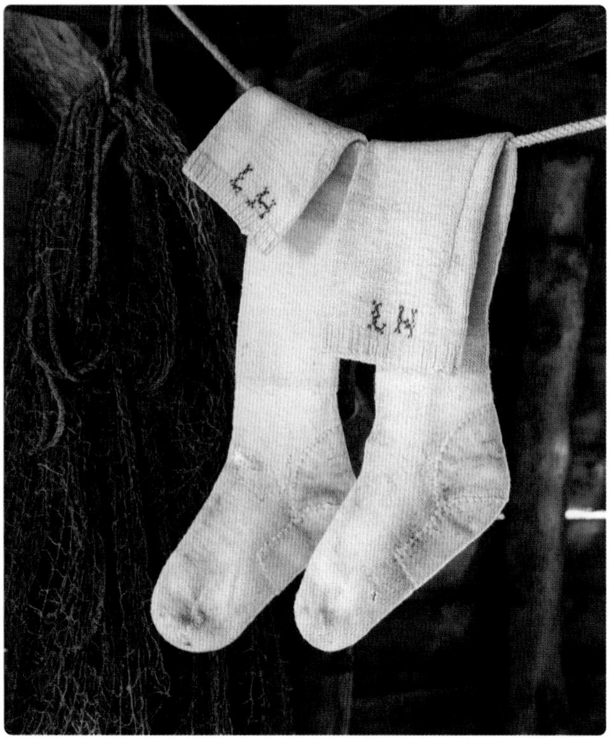

Photo: Kristin Støylen.

Handknitted stockings in natural white two-ply wool yarn. Stockinette with knit one, purl one—knit two, purl one ribbing. The legs are shaped at center back, and the feet end with round toes. The heels are reinforced with natural white, twill-woven wool fabric sewn on with natural white cotton thread, one piece over the other. The monogram "L H" is embroidered in cross stitch with two-ply red wool thread, on the right side of both stockings. The monogram is upside down.

Length from heel and up: 22¾ in / 58 cm

Width: 6¾ in / 17 cm

Width of ribbing: 1 in / 2.5 cm

Length, foot: 10¾ in / 27 cm

Shoe size: U. S. women's 12 or men's 9½ / Euro 43

Extra heel, inner piece: 3½ x 6¼ in / 9 x 16 cm and 3¾ x 6¼ in / 9.5 x 16 cm

Extra heel, outer piece: 4¾ x 4 in / 12 x 10 cm and 5¼ x 4¼ in / 13 x 11 cm

Length of monogram: 1 in / 2.7 cm

SEA MITTEN WITH MONOGRAM

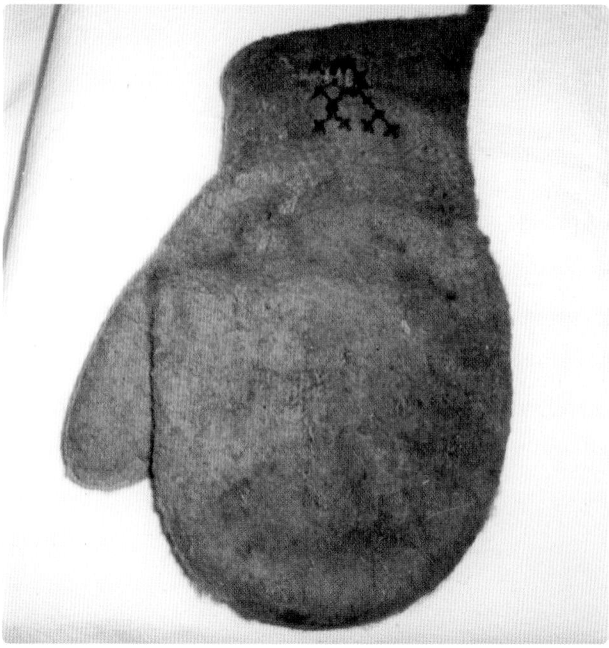

Photo: Sunnmøre Museum.

Handknitted, felted left-hand mitten from Leinøy. Stockinette without ribbing in gray-brown natural sheep's color, two-ply wool yarn. A braid is sewn securely into an opening so the mitten could be hung up. Embroidered monogram "A" in cross stitch with two-ply blue wool thread.

Length: 10¼ in / 26 cm

Width: 4¾ in / 12 cm

UNUSED SEA MITTENS

Photo: Kristin Støylen.

Handknitted sea mittens with natural white two-ply wool yarn. Stockinette with knit two, purl two ribbing. A braid is attached at the opening to hang up the mitten. Unused and not felted.

Length: 13 in / 33 cm

Width: 6 in / 15.5 cm

Width of ribbing: 2⅜ in / 6 cm

Length of thumb: 4¾ in / 12 cm

Width of thumb: 2½ in / 6.5 cm

Length of braid: 6 in / 15.5 cm

RED HAT

Photo: Kristin Støylen.

Handknitted hat in stockinette, with red two-ply handspun wool yarn; the same yarn is used for the whole hat. The folded brim at the lower edge is sewn down to the hat. Small loops are sewn onto the upturned brim in rows, with each row sewn over two stitches in width. The tassel is damaged and sewn onto the hat.

Length: 12¾ in / 32 cm

Width: 10¼ in / 26 cm

Width of looped band: 1⅝ in / 4 cm

Length of tassel: 1¾ in / 4.5 cm

LEATHER SKIRT

Photo: Kristin Støylen.

This leather skirt from Ørskog was sewn by hand in primary sections. The top part consists of two skins, with the neck skin extending down towards the wrists. The sewn-on skirt is a whole skin on the front and two leather pieces at the back. The section seams are sewn with double rows of stitches, and the rest with single rows of stitching. The sleeves and lower edge of the skirt have raw edges, without a hem. The triangular chest flap with a button is cut high enough at the back neck that it makes a collar, and then is lengthened with one piece on each side as a front band. This piece is 3¼ in / 8 cm wide at the back neck, tapering down to ¾ in / 2 cm at the split on the chest. At Sunnmøre, they only used calf skin for the seams.

Length: 28¾ in / 73 cm

Width: 32¾ in / 82 cm

Length from sleeve to sleeve: 64¼ in / 163.5 cm

Width of sleeve: 11¾ in / 30 cm

Length of skirt: 14¾ in / 37.5 cm

Width of neck: 9 in / 23 cm

Length of neck placket: 3½ in / 9 cm

Diameter of button: 1 in / 2.5 cm

Weight: 2.9 pounds / 1.3 kilos

LEATHER PANTS

Photo: Kristin Støylen.

These leather pants from Stranda were sewn by hand in primary sections that go down to the knees. The pants were sewn from two skins, one for each leg. All the seams on the pants are doubled except for the bands, which have three rows of stitches. Sewn together on the inside of the legs. Joined into one piece at the lower edge of both legs and on the back edge of pants to make a curve at the top. Twisted leather cords are sewn as loops on the inside under the back band, so the pants can be hung up. The waistband, with a long split at the front, is closed with a sewn-on belt buckle on the right side and sewn-on belt end on the left. The edges of the split and the pants legs are raw, without a hem.

Length: 19 in / 48.5 cm
Width, top: 16⅛ in / 41 cm
Length, leg from crotch: 17⅛ in / 43.5 cm
Width of leg at lower edge: 15 in / 38 cm
Length of split: 9 in / 23 cm
Width of waistband: 1⅛ in / 3 cm
Length of belt buckle: 1⅜ in / 3.5 cm
Width of belt buckle: 1 in / 2.5 cm
Length of buckle end: 6 in / 15 cm
Length of belt end: 6 in / 15 cm

SMALL BOOTS

Photo: Kristin Støylen.

Three pairs of small *røyserter* boots of ox or cow leather, all pairs handsewn with leg, heel, and top. The backs of the boots have small pieces sewn on, from the heel up to the top of the leg, to hide and reinforce the join underneath, with a loop at the top of each piece to help pull the boots on and to hang them up. The two largest pairs are alike. The largest pair, however, has legs made with two horizontal pieces of skin, machine-sewn together. The top piece also has decorative seams sewn on by machine. All three pairs have soles and heels. The two largest pairs have wooden soles, cut out in one whole piece. One pair has one layer of leather reinforcement, attached with wooden nails. The smallest pair has soles of glued layers with leather attached to the boot with wooden nails.

Height: 14⅜ in / 36.7 cm
Length: 13 in / 33 cm
Shoe size: Men's U. S. 17 / Euro 52
Width of last: from seam to seam: 7½ in / 19 cm
Width of boot leg: 7½ in / 19 cm
Height of heel: 1⅝ in / 4 cm
Height of sole: 1⅛ in / 3 cm
Weight of pair: 5.9 lbs / 2.7 kg

Height: 14⅜ in / 36.5 cm
Length: 12½ in / 31.5 cm
Shoe size: Men's U. S. 15 / Euro 50
Width of last: from seam to seam: 7 in / 18 cm
Width of boot leg: 8¼ in / 21 cm
Height of heel: 1⅜ in / 3.5 cm
Height of sole: 1⅛ in / 3 cm
Weight of pair: 4.4 lbs / 2 kg

Height: 13½ in / 34.5 cm
Length: 11½ in / 29 cm
Shoe size: Men's U. S. 12 / Euro 46
Width of last: from seam to seam: 6¾ in / 17 cm
Width of boot leg: 8 in / 20 cm
Height of heel: 1⅝ in / 4 cm
Height of sole: ⅜ in / 1 cm
Weight of pair: 3.3 lbs / 1.5 kg

LEATHER HAT

Photo: Kristin Støylen.

Handmade leather hat with core of gray heather wool felt. The leather is drawn over a thick felt hat. The crown is made with two skins, and the brim with one skin on the outside and two on the inside. Sewn on the right side with two narrow leather strips. The hat has a leather edge with two leather earflaps at the back, with holes for ties which are now missing.

Diameter, outer: 12¾-13½ in / 32.5-34.5 cm
Diameter, inner: 7-8 in / 18-20 cm
Length of crown: 13-13½ in / 33-34.5 cm
Width of brim: 3 in / 7.5 cm
Length of earflaps: 2⅜ and 2¾ in / 6 and 7 cm
Weight: 15.9 oz / 450 g

ELEMENTS OF THE GARMENTS FROM INNERMOST TO OUTERMOST

If you gather all these sources together, you'll come up with the full list of clothing below, in order from innermost to outermost. These garments were worn together in various combinations. The designation "shirt" (*skjørte*) often referred to an upper-body garment, though not quite like the piece of clothing we call a shirt today. Most outer garments were closed at the front, and pulled on over the head. Wool was innermost to hold in warmth, and was just as important as the outermost leather layer, which repelled water.

Garments for the top of the body

Under-sweater (shirt)
In-between sweater (shirt)
Over-shirt
Knitted pullover
Work blouse (*busserull*)
Breast cloth
Vest
Leather sleeves
Vadmal or leather strips to wrap wrists
Knitted wrist warmers
Sea mittens
Cap
Leather hat
Scarf
Sea sweater
Jacket
Leather skirt
Apron

Garments for the lower body

Inner-stockings
Over-stockings
Stocking bands
Under-pants
Top-pants
Outer-pants
Sea boots

Garments for the Top of the Body

UNDER-SWEATER (SHIRT)

Both fisher-farmers and inland farmers wore white wool shirts nearest the body. The oldest shirts were made of woven wool in primary pieces, and their shaping was the same all along the coast. Women and men wore the same type of undershirt, and while women's wool shirts were shorter in most areas of Norway, they were long and loose-fitting, like a slip, in coastal areas. Men's shirts went down to the knees. These shirts were not completely joined at the underarms, but had an open split so that sweat could drain off. They also had a short split at the sides on the lower part of the shirt, and most had tight neck openings with a small split. In coastal districts, wool shirts had a *kvare*, which is a small edging around the neck and chest placket. The sleeves were edged with canvas.

Around 1850, sleeves became wider and gained cuffs at the wrists, influenced by fashion, in the fjords and further inland; but in coastal areas, wool shirts were still made with smooth sleeves without cuffs. Around the same time, most wool shirts acquired front bands and buttons instead of an open split, and this change, by contrast, also appeared on shirts along the Norwegian coast. These front bands were either wool or canvas, and buttons were sewn onto the right side. Sweaters with long sleeves in the Sunnmøre Museum have such front bands. Later, it became common to sew buttons onto the left side.

In the 1860s, it became common to weave the body of the shirt but knit the sleeves. This represented a great advancement; these shirts were more comfortable to work in. The body was still made with *vadmal* for protection on sea journeys, and people began to sew a double layer of fabric over the shoulders as reinforcement.

The last change was to shift to knitting the entire under-shirt, and to full it to make it firmer and more durable. One under-sweater with long sleeves in the Sunnmøre Museum is an example of this style of garment: totally knitted, fulled, with front bands with buttons on the right side. While these knitted sweaters became very common, there were still older fishermen who wore sweaters with a *vadmal* body in the 1950s. A common feature of the wool shirts of old and the later knitted under-sweaters was the color—white—and the way they were worn, tucked down into the trousers.[36]

IN-BETWEEN SWEATER

Fishermen wore a wool or *vadmal* in-between sweater over their under-sweaters, and they might have worn two or three such in-between sweaters at the same time. According to Iver Ancher Heltzen, one of these sweaters was often a sheepskin sweater with wool on it. The in-between garments of *vadmal* were called wool shirts (*ullskjorter*), as Hans Strøm also wrote. They went down to the hip and were worn outside the trousers, with or without a belt, or tucked into the waistband. Even if the garment was called a shirt, it was a closed sweater, which was pulled on over the head. Wool shirts were primarily shaped with straight side seams without gussets, as for under-sweaters, and were dyed red or blue.[37]

OVER-SHIRT

On top of the white under-sweater and any in-between sweaters, fishermen wore a dyed shirt of woven wool, which was also closed up the front. Information about the division of estates in Vestland from 1695 to the beginning of the nineteenth century reveals that these shirts were red. Later on, blue over-shirts were also worn. This shirt could have variations in silhouette, and the neckline could be as wide as needed to easily pull the shirt on over the head. At the beginning of the nineteenth century, necklines became tighter, and these shirts tended to feature a chest split and chest placket with three buttons. The shirts had a low standing collar, and sleeves with cuffs and buttons. The classic solid red color stayed popular, but from 1850 to 1910, the most common over-shirts were striped or checked pattern fabrics. Preserved samples show great variation, originality, and pleasure in color combinations. On Sundays, when fishermen were on land, they wore yet another shirt over their over- and under-shirts. This was a canvas shirt, which was either white or had bright stripes.[38]

KNITTED PULLOVERS

In the 1850s, knitted pullovers began to substitute for one layer of in-between sweaters. In Vestland, they wore knitted pullovers, also called "nightshirts" or "night sweaters" (*nattrøyer*), over their white under-shirts. It is unclear whether these nightshirts were worn instead of an over-shirt or in addition to it. The name "nightshirt" might make you think that it was a garment worn only at night, but it wasn't. The name "nightshirt" was used for knitted household garments worn in towns from the end of the sixteenth century into the seventeenth century. The original "nightshirts" were continental and exclusive, preferably produced with expensive materials such as silk and embellished with gold embroidery. Later, the same term was used for knitted pullovers from the Vestland coast up to Lofoten. These sweaters didn't have a chest split on fishermen's garments, and were pulled on over the head.

Trætteberg wrote that a well-dressed young man in Øygarden outside Bergen would have three knitted sweaters with different patterns. For everyday wear, he'd have a sweater with a simple pattern—stripes, for example, or spots (called "lice"). In this case, striping would alternate between a narrow blue stripe and a wider white stripe, and the white stripes had blue spots. Today, we recognize this stripe sequence as the Fana pattern. Another example was a black and white sweater with blocks of clover patterns. The blocks were black

No rule without an exception. This is Roman Karpwitch, photographed in 1884. He is wearing a knitted sweater with a split. The main color is white, and the stripes, red. We can also see that he's wearing a shirt, possibly canvas, and a knitted sweater underneath, which is similar to the knitted pullover, with red and white stripes that look like they're the same width. Karpwitch was Sami (*skoltesame*) and a fisherman. He lived in Boris Gleb, a country village on the west side of Pasvik River, the Russian side, right on the border with Norway. Photo: G. Roche, Prince Roland Bonaparte/Musée de l'Homme. Colorization: Per Ivar Somby.

and white, and every other block had five points. For church, or other special occasions when he wanted to dress up, this young man would have a sweater with larger motifs and eight-petal roses. Øygarden had these large-pattern sweaters shipped in from areas of Hardanger, and people who lived along the coast ordered them or shopped for them when they came in by boat to buy wood.

Simpler patterns were also used for what we in Norway today call "Icelanders" (*Islender*) or "Icelandic sweaters." At that time, Icelanders were white with red spots, or sheep's black with red spots and white lower sections. According to village traditions, sweaters with small repeating patterns were older than those with large patterns such as eight-petal roses, which became the style in the 1840s-1850s, with the body and sleeves knitted in two-color patterns. As a general rule, the colors were sheep's black and white. The top part of the sweater body featured variations on eight-petal roses, diagonal crosses, blocks, and squares. The lower part of the sweater body, called the *bråtet*, was white, because it was tucked into the trousers and wouldn't be seen—so it wasn't necessary to knit the entire sweater with patterns and dyed yarn. Pattern-knitted sweaters were hugely popular, and a wide variety of different motifs and designs were developed by women making their own variations of patterns already in circulation and in use. It was a way to display one's creativity, joy in handwork, and skill.[39]

The diagonal cross was called an Andrew's cross, because the apostle Andrew died on a cross shaped like an X. Andrew's cross was very frequently used in Norwegian knitting patterns. It symbolizes humility; the shape of the cross is said to have been altered at Andrew's request, because he didn't want to die on a cross exactly like the one Jesus had been nailed to. The eight-petal rose has been used in ornamentation all around the world. It is richly symbolic, and used to embellish everything from knitting and filigree to ceramics, as well as wall and floor coverings. Blocks or squares are found in a number of regions and often symbolize the four corners of the world.[40]

WORK BLOUSE (*BUSSERULL*)

Fishermen wore work blouses under their sea-sweaters when fishing, and, in good weather, could row in just a work blouse and leather sleeves. The garment was pulled on over the head and worn over the pants. These blouses were made of gray *vadmal* or half-wool fabric, with gray cotton warp and blue and black wool weft. During the summer, fishermen wore blue and white striped cotton tops. In Troms, the *busserull* was called a *pusseronk*, and might also be made of sailcloth.[41]

BREAST CLOTH

A breast cloth was a *vadmal* body without sleeves, worn over the white under-shirt and dyed over-shirt. It had a short slit at the neck that was closed with a breast flap and buttons. Preserved garments are red, blue, and green, lined with tow. Tow is the short, coarse fiber removed when processing flax for linen spinning: hackled flax has long fibers. Tow is a waste product that was carded and spun as for wool and used for, among other items, toweling and coarser everyday clothing. The breast cloth went down over the hips and was tucked into the pants when a fisher-farmer was at sea. When he was on land, he wore it loose outside his pants with a belt around the waist. This was an old clothing item that fishermen held onto long after vests became common to wear when on land. A breast cloth was more comfortable for them to wear than a vest, which had many buttons that caught in the seine and nets. The breast cloth was also warmer and better than a vest and, in Hordaland, old fishermen wore them all the way to 1900.[42]

VEST

It became the modern fashion to wear a vest instead of a breast cloth when fishing; early on in the development of this trend, these vests still had a *vadmal* back, as on a breast cloth. The vest was worn over the white under-shirt and dyed over-shirt, exactly like a breast cloth. In northern Norway, vests were entirely gray or dark blue. Vests had single buttoning until the style changed to double buttoning. There was no band at the neck, or, if there was one, it had a low standing collar as for the over-shirt.[43]

LEATHER SLEEVES

Leather sleeves were made of fine skin from the belly of a goat, and reached from the wrist to above the elbow. Leather sleeves were especially worn when fishermen pulled in their nets. They would remove their leather skirts and pull leather sleeves on over their work blouses or *vadmal* sweaters instead, because that made it easier to perform the body movements their work tasks required.

VEVLINGER (WRIST WRAPS)

Vevlinger were long strips of vadmal or leather for wrapping the wrists. They were useful for keeping warm and protecting the wrists. Fishermen often got "sea pox" when out fishing—this was their name for boils that formed on the wrists and underarms due to chafing and sea water. Fabric strips used for *vevlinger* had to be undyed; otherwise dye would seep into these wounds. The strips were usually 4-6 in / 10-15 cm wide and 15¾-31½ in / 40-80 cm long, and were wrapped up over the arms. *Vevlinger* for wear at sea had to be soft, without hard edges or folds that could chafe the skin, and *vadmal* strips had only trimmed edges without being folded in. In the 1880s, knitted *vevlinger* came into vogue. They were knitted on two needles in garter stitch and were also undyed. Knitted strips were also worn for more formal outfits, but these were dyed.[44]

WRIST WARMERS

Beginning in the 1860s, people in Hordaland wore knitted wrist warmers instead of *vevlinger.* The term *vevling*, or *foreme* ("forearm"), was primarily reserved for wrist warmers used when at sea. Wrist warmers were 6-8 in / 15-20 cm long, and worked in knit and purl ribbing so they fitted closely around the wrists. If a fisherman had sea pox, it was uncomfortable to wear a white *vadmal* undershirt edged with canvas. These edges easily felt hard and painful when they chafed against injured wrists. So women began knitting wrist warmers of fine wool yarn that could be sewn onto *vadmal* sleeves. These wrist warmers were 2¾-3¼ in / 7-8 cm long, with knit 1, purl 1 ribbing, with a few rounds of stockinette first. Two of the knitted sweaters in the Sunnmøre Museum have such ribbing.[45]

SEA MITTENS

Sea mittens were a very important part of fishermen's outfits. They were a fisherman's work mittens, and protected his hands against cold, injuries from fishing tools, and the knife during gutting. Without healthy hands, it was difficult to row and fish. Sea mittens were worked as *lovott*, a term for the style that is now standard: the hand and fingers had a place in the mitten hand, while the thumb was covered separately. There were also sea mittens with two thumbs, used from a little before the 1850s onward. They were called "two-thumb mittens" (*to-tomlingsvette*). This type of mitten had the advantage of being wearable on either hand. When one thumb was worn out, the mitten could be turned and worn on the other hand, so the second thumb could be used. These mittens were made with undyed wool, because that was thought to be warmer than dyed wool, and they were knitted many sizes too big so they could be fulled properly. They might be fulled beforehand and would still be too big, but that wasn't a problem for long; some women didn't bother fulling them in advance at all, as they would shrink quickly in seawater. Sea mittens were produced to tolerate particularly hard use, and had to be thick to protect the hands. This on-the-job fulling process meant that all-too-big sea mittens would only become thicker as they were worn. It was said that a finished mitten could be up to a half yard/meter long, and have a thumb so large that one could fit a whole fist in it. One of Trætteberg's interviewees said that, in 1961, when he was little, he could fit his whole lower body in one of his father's line-hauling mittens.

Sources inform us that fishermen had up to five pairs of mittens when they went out to fish, and mittens were an absolute necessity for which there was no substitute. There were two types of sea mittens for fishing. One (called *vavotter*) was for hauling in line and nets, as well as gutting the fish. The word *vad* means "line" or "angle cord." These mittens had to be strong, because they were exposed to very hard wear and tear. The second type, "rowing mittens" (*rovotter*), were worn when fishermen rowed. These had to be warm and were made with pure wool, the best lamb's wool—long, soft wool spun loosely and thickly.

Something that might sound a bit strange to us today is that fishermen always wet their mittens first, when they had to row out to fish or draw in nets. This, of course, was a well-considered decision: wet mittens held in body heat, so the fishermen counter-intuitively avoided cold hands by making sure their mittens were wet. These mittens certainly live up to the name "sea mittens"! When evening came, and the fisherman was finished for the day, he rinsed his sea mittens in the sea before slapping them against a rock and trampling on them. After this treatment, the mittens were hung up in the boathouse. There, they froze overnight, and the next morning, the fisherman would dip them in the sea to thaw them. If they were laid on the boat seat, he could sit on them while he rowed. That way, they were no longer frozen when he pulled them on. Rowing mittens might also be dipped in sea water before the fisherman put them on. On Hitra, by contrast, they kept their fishing mittens in the boat after fishing, and had other ways to thaw them the next day. If the mittens were wet or had been used for gutting, they were trampled down into the snow or in the sea to rinse off the blood. They were then twisted up and laid on the boat frame, where each man had his space on the boat. The next day, the stiffly frozen mittens were bound with cord and hung over the boat's gunwale and down into the sea. The mittens thawed there until the fishermen could put them on.[46]

Monogram on sea stockings. Photo: Kristin Støylen.

After knitting sea mittens and stockings, women embroidered them with the owner's initials in cross stitch on the garments. That made it easy for each man to find his own mittens and stockings, when everyone had hung up their clothes to dry or in the boathouse.

Nålbinding ("needle weaving") is a stitching technique with a needle and wool yarn, practiced in many parts of the world. The technique was very common in Norden in the Middle Ages (approximately 500-1500 CE). Knitting is a much newer technique that eventually took over from nålbinding, as it was much easier to knit with needles than to sew with a needle. A knitted cotton sock was found in Egypt, dated to somewhere between the 1100s and 1300s. It has a white background, and geometric patterning in white and blue in panels. Knitting spread from there and became very popular in Europe by the sixteenth century; it was considered common in Norway in the seventeenth to eighteenth centuries. Nålbound mittens and stockings were worn for fishing before that point, but by the 1700s to 1900s, these garments were knitted, despite the belief that nålbound garments were warmer and more durable than knitted ones.

STOCKING CAP

Knitted red stocking caps, like the one in Sunnmøre Museum's collections, have a long history in Norway. These caps were common headgear for fishermen along the whole coast in the nineteenth century, and were also very often worn by inlanders. Today, these caps are often part of Norwegian national and folk costumes. Oral tradition relates that, for the most part, people in Nordland and Troms preferred red stocking caps to caps of other colors. They called the red caps *rølue* in these regions, and in Sunnmøre, *raudelue*. Other sources indicate that such caps were worn earlier than the 1800s. A glass painting from Bergen in 1700 shows a farmer wearing a red stocking cap while he plays a clarinet. The artist, Jørgen Christensen Garnaas (1723-1798), carved a wooden statue of a fisherman from Borgund on Sunnmøre in about 1750; this wooden fisherman is wearing a leather outfit and red stocking cap with a blue pile edging. In Nordmannsdalen, in the castle park of Fredensborg Palace in Denmark, there is a statue from the 1760s showing a man from Akershus with a stocking cap. These red caps typically had a dyed brim at the lower edge in blue, green, or yellow, or striped in several colors. The lower edge could also be covered in pile—short strands of yarn knotted under the knitting. The strands were cut to the desired length first by wrapping the yarn around a small dowel, so all the strands could be cut to the same

This is Ellend Ellingsen Hole (born in 1814) with his wife, Gunhild, and their three daughters, photographed in Geiranger in 1869. Hole had moved to Geiranger from Sunnylven, and is wearing a striped knitted sweater, long white knitted stockings, and a red cap. The English photographer was very much taken with Hole's stocking cap, and Hole told him that he had had the cap for 33 years, and that means he got the cap when he was 22 years old. Photo: Edward Backhouse Mounsey (1840-1911). Owner: National Library.

length.[47] The same technique was used to prepare pile for pile rugs or boat ryas. The pile edge could also be made in other ways.

These red stocking caps were worn under a leather hat when fishing, and later under a sou'wester. The tip of the stocking cap folded over to the right side, so that the tassel covered the ear, and the cap could be pulled down well over the forehead. The custom of wearing a red cap varied over time. In Øygarden, fishermen wore them all the way up until 1900, while in Rana, the custom was already dying out among the young by 1834.

One interviewee told Trætteberg

> In Øygarden in Hordaland, the rule was that when a boy became three years old, he got a stocking cap. From that time, he wore it day and night through his manhood and old age. And when, on the big day, he stood before our Lord, he also had to be wearing the stocking cap. It went with him to his casket. At night, he wore his cap, although he was otherwise naked in bed.[48]

Besides the traditional red stocking cap, fishermen also wore patterned caps, called rose caps (*roseluer*) on the Bergen coast (the western coast of Norway). This term was used regardless of whether the pattern was actually eight-petal roses, blocks, diagonal crosses, or other geometric motifs. Caps with patterning were also worn in the coastal areas of Trøndelag and Hordaland in the nineteenth century. They had wide panels of geometric patterns in many colors, and, as for knitted sweaters, women adapted motifs to their own tastes and personalized them. Rose caps were worked in knit stitch with two-ply wool yarn. The background color was dark blue, or occasionally, red-brown. Every main panel in the pattern had lines with narrow hook and block borders. The crown of the cap was knitted with a rounded shaping and the tassel was made with the remaining colors of the cap.[49] By this time, the colors could be a mixture of plant and chemical dyes,[50] so a cap could have a strong contrast of bright and pale colors. Imagine what fantastic and exciting color combinations these knitted caps and sweaters must have had!

LEATHER HAT

Both pictorial and written sources from the eighteenth and nineteenth centuries show and tell us that fishermen wore leather hats. Preserved leather hats are of two sorts. One is the so-called *våsehatt*, worn in Hordaland, with a wide brim and low crown. They were made only of leather. The other type was a leather hat with a lining of felt, as is preserved in the Sunnmøre Museum. This type was part of the fishermen's outfit, and was made with the same shaping all along the Norwegian coast. These leather hats were 14¼ in / 36 cm in diameter. As a general rule, the crown was 4 in / 10 cm high, and the width of the brim from the crown to the edging was 2¾ in / 7 cm. The leather hat in the Sunnmøre Museum is 12⅞-13½ in / 32.5-34.5 in diameter—it isn't symmetrically round. The length of the crown is 13-13½ in / 33-34.5 cm if you measure from the seam, over the top, and down to the seam on the other side. Divided by two, it measures approximately 6½ in / 16.5 cm. The brim is 3 in / 7.5 cm wide.

A tanned sheep or goat skin was used for a hat, and the top of the brim had to be a single piece of uncut leather so water could easily run off. It didn't matter whether the piece of leather on the underside of the brim was cut, however, as the hat at the Sunnmøre Museum shows. It was important to use the skin as efficiently as possible so nothing was wasted; therefore, the underside could consist of 3-4 pieces of leather. The leather pieces on the hat were secured with glue made from halibut roe, and then sewn together with strips of goatskin. Earflaps were made of soft *vadmal* or block-patterned cotton fabric, and sewn securely to the felt inside the hat. Braided wool cords in many colors were used for ties attached to the ends of the earflaps. For example, the cord might be red and gray, as a colorful feature set off by all the leather. The hat in the Sunnmøre Museum has leather earflaps with a hole at the end of each flap to show where there would have been a tie. The leather hats were both tight and warm, but they were also heavy. A hat often weighed over 1.1 lb / half a kilo—which was actually an advantage, when the fisherman bowed his head into the breakwaters and sea wind. The leather hat at Sunnmøre Museum weighs almost 1.1 lb / .5 kg.[51]

In Nordland and Troms, fishermen wore leather headgear similar to a southwester (sou'wester). This was called a *sjyhætta* ("sea hood") or *sjyhatt* ("sea hat"). The oldest leather sea hoods reached into the leather skirt and hung like a straight shirttail down the back.[52]

WOOL SCARF

We haven't found any old sources that specifically mention what knitted wool scarves looked like, or whether they were made here in Norway. In Iceland and the Faroe Islands, it was common to choose soft, natural sheep's colors for scarf wool. Fine wool was considered the warmest, and undyed wool warmer than dyed wool. Although scarves are not specially mentioned in our sources, we think they were worn in Norway, and there was probably nothing in particular that would have set them apart from Icelandic or Faroese scarves in their technique or look.

SEA JACKET

Sea jackets made with *vadmal* were common travel and fishing garments, often worn for local fishing but not on the high sea. For local fishing, fishermen preferred sea jackets rather than leather skirts. These jackets closed at the front and were pulled on over the head like sweaters. Men all along the coast wore sea jackets, which had the same general style, although there were local variations in shaping. The silhouette was primarily straight, with curved side seams but not gussets, as for wool shirts. The farmer's daily sweater and *vamp* had gussets. Sea jackets were worn from 1750 until the 1830s and, in some areas, up until 1900.[53]

VAMP

A *vamp* is an overgarment, a type of jacket made with *vadmal*, with an open front that reaches down to the middle of the thighs. It's unclear whether this garment was worn under the leather skirt or only as a single garment when fishing locally.[54]

LEATHER SKIRT

Wearing a leather skirt was a necessity when fishing on the high seas. The garment was time-consuming to make and expensive to buy, and those who didn't have the means for a leather skirt had to use vadmal. The importance of the leather skirt meant greater demands on the garment. Everything was well-planned, from how to cut the skin to where the seams should be placed. This was important for the entire leather outfit. Skins were cut so the strongest parts were placed where the garment was most likely to be exposed to wear, tear, and water. Seams were stitched as tightly as possible so water couldn't penetrate them. Three

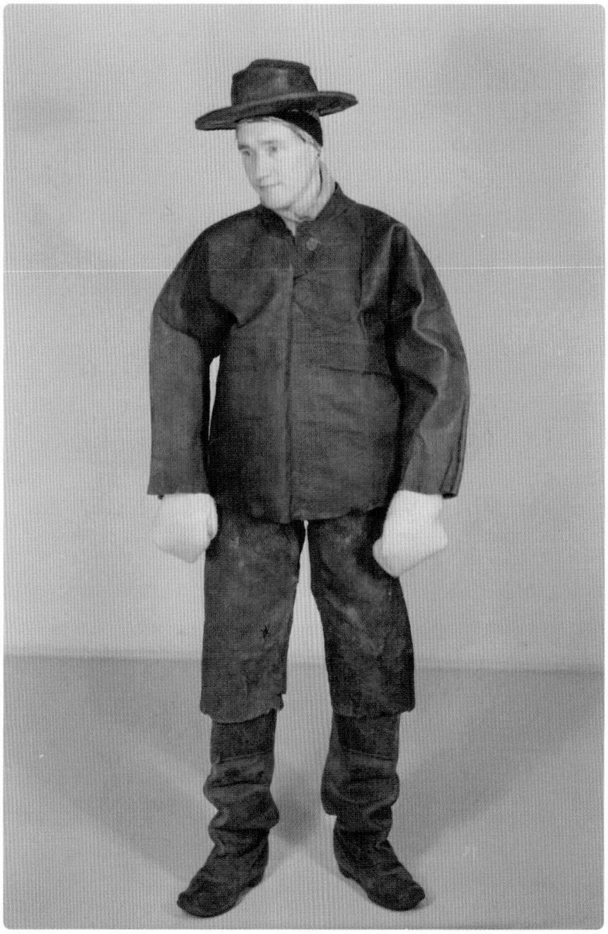

Leather outfit in the Sunnmøre Museum. Photo: Norsk Folkemuseum.

to four skins were needed for a skirt, depending on the size of the body it would cover and what animal the skin came from. The shaping of the leather skirt required a top section reaching from the base of the man's throat to the lowest rib, and covering a corresponding area of the back. At the same time, the top part covered the arms, and was made of two large pieces of leather, with two small pieces lower on the sleeves to provide enough width. The seam was vertical at the center of the chest and on the center back, and the top was securely sewn to a so-called "skirt." This skirt was formed by rectangular pieces on the body below the seams. The front skirt had to be stronger to protect from water coming off of lines and nets, so there was never a seam placed in the center of the lap. The skirt was attached to the top section with a horizontal seam that continued out and joined the sleeves in a "cut seam." Some leather skirts had square underarm gussets for more ease and comfort. The vertical seams on the back and chest were cut seams, worked the same way on all leather skirts no matter where along the coastline they were made. These seams were always made with a double row of stitches, because this was where the garment stretched the most. Otherwise, both leather skirts and trousers were sewn with a single row of small running stitches. In some seams—for example, the inside of the legs and the crotch of the pants—a double row of stitches was used. Sometimes these clothes had folded seams from sewing down leather pieces that had been doubled over to make them the right size for the actual garment. The size of the pieces and the placement of seams varied depending on the size of the skin. The strips used for sewing were made from kid, year-old goat (*risbit*), cat, or dog. *Risbit* is the word for a young ram or goat buck. The leather skirt in the Sunnmøre Museum was sewn following these templates.[55]

APRON

When a fisherman had to gut fish,[56] he protected himself with a leather apron. On Sunnmøre, this apron was called a *bringeskinn*, and in northern Norway, a *fangskinn*. It was common to wear a whole skin, but preserved items also show aprons made from several pieces. In Mo i Rana, aprons were worn for fishing up to the 1880s and 1890s. At that time, fishermen had two leather aprons: one worn on the front of the body and the other on the back. That way, a fisherman could stay dry while sitting on the boat seat, and at the same time be protected against water when he drew in lines or did deep fishing with a hand line. In essence, two aprons functioned as a substitute for a leather skirt.[57]

Garments for the Lower Body

WOOL STOCKINGS

Foot coverings, such as stockings and socks, have many different names in the various districts of Norway; materials and techniques also varied. Knitted stockings were already being made in Norway in the sixteenth century, when knitting was also popular in Europe. For fishing, men wore two pairs of wool stockings: inner stockings and outer stockings. A fisherman needed 4 pairs of inner stockings and 2-3 pairs of outer stockings when he left for a season's fishing. In many places, the customary look was black stockings with white toes, and one would sew on an extra heel in gray *vadmal* to reinforce the heel against wear.

Inner stockings were worn innermost, against the skin, and went up to the knees or even higher. In Troms, inner stockings were knitted with gray three-ply Spelsau wool yarn, which was considered the best and warmest wool for sea wear. Some examples of extant stockings have 2¾-3 in / 7-8 cm of ribbing, with the rest of the stocking in stockinette, plus shaping on both sides of the leg. The heel is decreased at the center under the foot, and the toe is flat with decreases on two sides. Monograms were embroidered in cross stitch using red or blue wool yarn. Finally, braided cords were added so a pair of stockings could be tied together and hung up. The stockings at the Sunnmøre Museum are examples of this type of stocking, but with round toes and no point, unlike stockings from Troms. The stockings in the museum's collection also have heels reinforced with *vadmal*.

Over-stockings were pulled on over the inner stockings and went to the knees or the middle of the calf. They were knitted entirely in ribbing, because that made the stockings warmer than they would have been in only stockinette. The yarn was also thicker than that used for under-stockings. In Nordland, men wore over-stockings that went up to the middle of the thigh or up to the crotch, which were worn pulled on over *vadmal* pants.[58]

STOCKING BANDS

Stocking bands were also called hose bands, and were used to hold up stockings or hosiery. This item has been part of the daily dress code in Norway since early in the Middle Ages (500-1050 CE).[59] Stocking bands could be worn with or without knots. The band might be knotted below the knee, or wrapped twice around the leg with the end slipped under the band on the outside of the leg. Men also wore stocking bands to hold high boots in place. Stocking bands were worked with *bregda*, a braiding technique that made them more elastic than woven bands.[60]

UNDERPANTS

Underpants might be knitted in stockinette or worked in ribbing with white wool. Both types had tighter ribbing at the lower edges so the garment would sit closer to the body to hold in heat. Underpants had a sewn-on waistband and fly in natural-colored cotton canvas with 2-5 buttons on the right side, with one button on the waistband and the rest on the fly. The fly might also be knitted. In Nordland and Troms, it was common to wear handwoven underpants until knitting machines came into use.

OVER-PANTS

Over-pants were made with *vadmal* and were worn between the under- and outer trousers. Up to the middle of the nineteenth century, over-pants, or *brok* pants, reached the knees, and from 1850 on, it was common to wear long pants.

OUTER PANTS

Outer pants could be made of leather, sailcloth, canvas, or *vadmal*. The primary features of leather pants were such that they had the same styling all along the Norwegian coast, with smaller variations in cut. Variations were determined by the size and shape of the skins used. *Brok* pants were joined from a front and back piece on each leg with, as a rule, two skin pieces for each leg. The *brok* pants had a waistband and were cut higher at the back than the front. Most preserved leather pants have a split in the waistband on the right side, from the hip to 6-8 in / 15-20 cm down, but some also had a split at the front, as on the pants at the Sunnmøre Museum. *Brok* pants went approximately down to the knees, and the width at the lowest part of the pant legs was between 23¾-27½ in / 60-70 cm in order to allow a man to pull on his pants over his boots. The leather pants at the Sunnmøre Museum were made in this fashion.[61]

SEA BOOTS

In the eighteenth century, fishermen wore boots, while village men wore shoes. From the middle of the nineteenth century up to 1900, fishermen wore four types of leather boots of varying lengths: long boots, high boots, high-low boots (*røyserter*), and short *røyserter*. Sea boots were made of cow and ox skin, treated with a lubricant of boiled cod liver oil, tallow, and tar, and later blackened by various methods. In many districts of Norway, it was common to line sea boots with straw.

Long boots went up to the crotch and had two leather straps at the top edge that were attached to a belt at the waistband. These boots fit up inside leather pants, and were particularly worn during winter cod fishing.

High boots went up to about the middle of the thigh, but had the same shape as long boots. The top part of a high boot was made of softer leather, which could be folded down in a large cuff when not out on a boat. There was a loop on the inside of the boot, on each side of the kneecap; stocking bands could be pulled through these loops and wrapped around the leg to hold the boot in place. Both long boots and high boots were common along the coast from Rogaland to Troms in the eighteenth century, up to 1850, but even past that point, both types remained in use as long as fishermen went out in small boats, due to the need to wade into the water to pull a small boat onto land or push it out again.

Røyserter high-low boots came up to just below the kneecap. The Norwegian word *røysert* is derived from the phrase *å røyse opp*, "to pile up" or "to stand upright." These boots stood up by themselves, and didn't fall down the way long boots did. They had a short loop on the back of the leg to help when pulling them on, and could be bound together with these loops and hung up to dry.

Short *røyserter* boots were never higher than the middle of the calf, but could also be shorter. These boots had many names, one of which was *halfkannestøvler* ("half-*kanne* boots") because half a *kanne* (approximately two quarts/liters) fit into each boot. These small boots were light to carry, and were most often worn for local fishing. They came into fashion in the second half of the nineteenth century, at about the same time as longer *røyserter* boots.

A lithograph, "From Vandelven on Söndmör" by Georg C. C. Wedel Prahl, 1827-1832, shows a fisherman at left. He is wearing white stockings in folded-down high boots, held up by hose bands in loops at the knees, along with a red hat with blue edging and tassel, a scarf, a shirt, and leather sleeves. He carries a blue vest over his arm. But what is the garment with red, blue, and yellow stripes that he's wearing over his shirt? That garment is probably woven, as it has an entirely open front, and it looks like there is a pocket on the left side. Photo: Norsk Folkemuseum.

In Hordaland, men also wore *hylpastøvler,* which were sea boots that had wooden shoes with a high leather shaft, and were therefore also called wooden shoe boots. Two of the sea boots in the Sunnmøre Museum have soles made from a single piece of wood. In the coastal districts of Vestland, men wore clogs (*klogger*) while salting fish. These shoes had wooden soles and heels, with the shoe *vamp* tied at the front, and reached up over the calf. For cod fishing in Lofoten, fishermen preferred to take along a pair of wooden shoes. These would have been worn while in the shanty, when wet sea boots had been taken off. In Nordland and Troms, where Sami and other people lived together, fishermen wore stocking legs (*bellinger*) together with foot coverings of ox and sheep's skin filled with sedge grass. The stocking legs were made from a whole piece of goat skin shaped like a tube which was wound firmly around the leg with a strip from the ankle and up under the knee. These tubes were pulled on over vadmal pants and were especially worn for local fishing.[62]

Put together, it was something of a complicated outfit that fishermen wore, with layer upon layer of different garment elements for the upper and lower parts of the body and on the head. Now we understand that it was extremely important to ensure garments were functional, or a fisherman would end up with a heavily padded body that couldn't move easily. The materials used in fishermen's clothes were natural resources, and since these garments needed to be practical, it was important to find the right raw materials, to choose them well—and treat them with care. Keeping the animals that created these raw materials on the farm made them, for the most part, self-sufficient. Generations of experience had shown what parts of an animal had the best characteristics for various garments. Sheep were the most advantageous animals because of their wonderful wool, followed by goats and cattle. Most thought that sheep skins weren't fit for leather outfits, but they were used in some places anyway, perhaps because of a lack of availability of skins from other animals. Sheep, goats, and calves have skins with differing hair, and thus different characteristics; it was important to exploit those characteristics to advantage when making an outfit. Factors such as age, sex, conditions, and feed also influenced the quality of the skins. Fisher-farmers learned this from their forefathers and through their own experience. Goatskin was considered to be the most waterproof, so many fishermen preferred to use it for their whole outfit. Calfskin was used for pants, although in northern Norway, they also used reindeer and sealskin. All along the coast, sheepskin was thought to be the least waterproof, so it was used only for the catch piece in the skirt and for the upper arms.[63]

Domestic animals provided raw materials with qualities suitable for the various parts of a fisherman's outfit.

Sheep: under garments in-between garments, over garments, stockings, sea mittens, leather outfit, foot coverings, boat ryas
Goat: sea mittens, leather outfit, leather hat, leather sleeves, boot or stocking legs
Cow: sea boots
Ox: sea boots, foot coverings

MAKING THE CLOTHES—THE WORK OF A FAMILY

Ellen Kjellmo wrote that all research can lead to the easy conclusion that new discoveries and inventions came to us here in Norway from the larger world, and never the other way around. She referred to the question of boat ryas and their origins. Given that the need was there and the materials were available, it isn't unlikely that Norwegians found solutions for our particular needs on our own, rather than importing them from outside. After all, if there were anyone in the world driven to find a good way to keep themselves warm, it would have been men in our climate. Kjellmo wrote that East Asia has very old carpet traditions, but that rya-style rugs from that area and from Norden might have arisen in parallel. Both carpet traditions use the same kinds of knots, but these techniques are so easy that they can still plausibly have arisen in several places in the world independently of each other.[64] If we amend that first sentence to say "much research" and "rarely the other way around," then we're ready to get excited by what Kjellmo wrote. This framework is also valid for our research into fishermen's clothing, which is very much in the same category as boat ryas. Living conditions and weather conditions here in Norway are an obvious incentive for generations of trial and error in order to maximize functionality when making clothing and equipment, based on the preconditions and resources already available. Protective clothing for fishing was so vital to Norwegians' way of life for most of our history that solutions had to be found as early as possible.

Skins, wool, and flax were raw materials for clothing that people produced themselves on their farms, following unbroken traditions for centuries, all around the country. In the eighteenth century, cultivation of cotton from Indian seeds began on a large scale in North America, and the Industrial Revolution in England increased cotton production very quickly. By 1900, cotton led the world's textile market with an 80% share.[65] Throughout the nineteenth century, cotton replaced flax in many places in Norway. Cultivating and processing flax was very time-consuming, and it was easier and conferred status to buy fine imported cotton from England. However, there was no substitute for wool's excellent qualities, and small-scale local production of wool for textiles continued as a necessity throughout the nineteenth century for the fisher-farmer and his family. In most communities, women sewed clothing for the entire family, and among the peasant class, it was common for them to produce their own fabric also. Everyday clothing was made with wool, linen, and cotton yarn, woven into fabric at home. All undergarments and most outer garments were sewn at home, even after it gradually became common for tailors to travel from farm to farm and sew clothes for people. Nevertheless, most sewing was done by women on farms using home-made raw materials, something which left its mark on their working lives. Wool and linen were produced on the farm itself, and this work had to be planned. Up to the nineteenth century, most farms in Norway had a little flax field, and some also had a field of hemp. Flax was popular in the Middle Ages, and has maintained its great significance as a natural product even today. In Norway, flax cultivation just about ended completely at the end of the nineteenth century as cheap cotton gradually made it unfeasible to cultivate flax, with some local exceptions. On many farms, it was common to tan hides, whether to use for shoes and clothing on the farm, or to sell. There were also traveling shoemakers. Tradition suggested that boys should sew their own shoes for their church confirmation, and girls should sew their own dresses, almost as a journeyman's test in advance of starting a new family. Such knowledge was important to have in a marriage. The transition from producing one's own clothing in pre-industrial society to buying ready-made fabrics, and later finished clothing, must have been a bit of a revolution for the individual Norwegian woman who would previously have been responsible for all the textiles in her household. The county governor wrote in the beginning of the 1860s that "The Wool used for homemade Fabrics was exclusively cultivated at home, while purchased Machine-spun yarn for the most Part was used for weaving Cotton goods,"[66] which means people bought cotton yarn for weaving fabric at home. Even in 1760, Hans Strøm wrote that Norddal women wove such lovely fabric that it could be mistaken for purchased fabric; but in general, cotton fabric was not woven in large quantities until after 1835, when cotton yarn became cheaper.[67]

There was a clear division of work between women and men in households when it came to making the various parts of fishermen's outfits. Women took on all the work with wool, while the tanning, cutting, and sewing of leather garments were men's jobs. While men perfected leather outfits, women did the same with wool garments. Both parts were invaluable components of a fisherman's clothing, because it was important to stay both dry and warm. Children helped where they could, and so the knowledge of handwork was handed down from one generation to the next. There was also a division of work between fisher-farmers and specialists in the village. Fisher-farmers tanned most of the skins for their leather themselves, but got leather for the making of sea boots from specialists. In the nineteenth century, the sewing of sea boots was done by fisher-farmers themselves, or by village or town shoemakers; there was no sharp separation here between fisher-famers and shoemakers, and there were always shoemaking tools and lasts on the farm. On Senja, it was common for hired men to sew their own sea clothing and boots. Eilert Sundt wrote in 1867 that in Torsken, in Troms, there were 17 shoemakers who solely worked leather outfits and sea boots. Skins for leatherworking could also be sent to professional tanners, a production pathway that only really developed in Norway after the Craft Act was repealed in 1839. Up until then, it was illegal for handworkers to settle outside cities; with the repeal, they were allowed, among other things, to live on tenant tanneries in smaller villages.[68] Skins had to be tanned in order to transform the raw hide into watertight and durable leather that could easily be cut and sewn into clothes. Skins for fishermen's garments were traditionally tanned with bark, and so the process was called *barking*. Barking gave skins a yellow color, and took anywhere from nine months to a full year. First, the animal had to be slaughtered and skinned, and the skin preserved up until it was tanned. The hair had to be removed and the skin scraped clean before the tanning could be done. Finally, the skin had to be further processed by drying, and then machined with cutting and rubbing tools, lubricated, dyed, and softened. Then the resulting leather was ready to cut and sew into a garment. Skins were oiled on both sides with fish-liver oil, using a wool cloth, and some tanners also added a little tar to the mix for use on the inner side. Fish-liver oil was called "brightening" (*lyse*) in Norwegian, because it was also used for lightening.[69] Hat production was specialized work; felt-lined leather hats in particular were complicated to make, even if some fisher-farmers managed it themselves. In Rana, leather hats were not only made for use by local fishermen, but were also sold in Lofoten and other places, going under the name of *ranahatter*.[70] Fishermen's wives sewed sou'westers out of strong canvas, but by the 1890s, almost no one sewed these at home any longer. Already by 1867, 36,000 sou'westers were produced annually in Stavanger, demonstrating how quickly home production could be replaced by factory production.[71]

Autumn evenings were used for producing woolens for the winter fishing season; women spun yarn and knitted garments. Proficient girls could knit a pair of sea mittens over the course of a single evening. Sea boot socks were more difficult to knit, and took longer. At the same time, the men sat and made lines for home fishing, and made or mended nets. Everything that a fisherman needed had to be finished before the season began. The rest of the time, the work of producing textiles was spread over the whole year. The fisher-farmer's wife was responsible for spinning, weaving, knitting, and sewing everything needed for clothing and bedding for the whole family, and perhaps for a hired man and servant girl also. This work was formidable, and we can only attempt to understand how heavy it was. The months when the men were away for the winter fishing season were used for spinning, both early and late. During spring and summer, women wove fabric and sewed garments and bedclothes. During the fall, they oversaw the inventory and repaired and supplemented as needed. Wool garments were mended, patched, and repaired, while sea mittens and socks were purely expendable and had to be replaced every year. People knitted year-round; whenever they had a "free moment" on the way to the fields, the summer barn, or the neighbors' house, women and girls always had their knitting hooks on their belts and their knitting in their hands. Stocking caps were usually knitted by sweethearts and fishermen's wives. Fisher-farmers needed three of these caps: one for church, one to wear at home on the farm, and one for fishing. Fine handcrafts such as crochet and embroidery were "cozy" work, considered relaxing and saved for Saturday evenings and half-holidays.[72] They didn't have much reason to make nice things that weren't absolutely necessary. Fishermen's wives, as we discussed, had been criticized by local officials for having low standards and few pretty household items and embellishments, compared to those produced in inland communities. But how much time and how many resources did women along the coast have to spare for such activities—women who also had to do a farmer's work on top of their own, while the men were out fishing? We can see by looking at gifts given by sweethearts and weavings these women made that they had aesthetic sensibilities, too.

An additional factor in these communities where people, for the most part, made clothing at home was that unmarried men—for example, hired men—still needed to get clothes somewhere. This dilemma was solved with a custom by which it was common to pay hired workers with both money and clothing. Part of annual pay came in cash, with the rest as clothing, which had to last for a year or two. Clothing was both an important investment and, of course, a necessity. People didn't need to own their own home, but everyone had to have clothes. Since the process of making garments was quite time-consuming, paying part of someone's earnings in clothes was genuinely valuable. As a servant, a hired man wouldn't have a wife who could provide his clothing, and a servant girl had enough duties and work required by her employment already, so she didn't have time. There were large pay differences between the sexes—women earned much less than men. There were more servant girls than there were hired men, and hired men were in greater demand, so they were able to ask for higher compensation. Servant girls would probably not have had more value than hired men even if they'd been in the minority. In 1856-60, it was stated that a standard annual pay without clothing included was 20 spesidaler for a man and 10 spesidaler for a girl; annual pay with clothing was 12 spesidaler for a man and 4 spesidaler for a girl.[73] In 1859, Eilert Sundt wrote that "in the old days" an adult servant would receive a set of clothes every other year, which was part of their pay for that two-year period. This set of clothes included:

> Pants and jackets of *vadmal* fabric 8 *alen* long (about 16 feet / 4.9 meters),[74] completely sewn but without buttons, 2 shirts, 1 pair of new and 1 pair knitted hose, 1 pair of mittens, 1 hat or cap, [and] finally, a few marks of leather, which the man, like every other man, could with his own hands use to sew shoes for himself.[75]

This set was valued at 5 spesidaler. In the 1850s, it became more common to get the entire year's pay in cash. That meant that men had to acquire their own clothes, and they had to make do with 5-7 spesidaler for clothing for two years. One reason for this could be that, from 1850 onward, it was more expensive to pay part of a year's earnings in clothing—simply because they took more fabric. Styles had changed so that men no longer went about in knee breeches but instead wore long pants, and women's skirts were considerably longer, too. By paying the entire year's earnings in cash, the farmer avoided losing out due to these new fashions.

Another factor was that most men who rowed out fishing paid for the equipment they needed, but not everyone was able to acquire a full set of fishermen's clothing. For example, they wore *vadmal* clothing instead of a leather outfit, and used sheepskin instead of boat ryas. Eilert Sundt wrote that in Haram in the 1860s, servant men went out fishing at their own expense, but their masters provided them with their leather outfits; they got borrowed sea boots, leather skirts, and leather pants. In 1788, Hans Strøm calculated how much each piece of a set of fishing garments cost, and he found that one leather skirt made of goatskin cost 1 riksdaler and 3 marks, leather pants cost 5 marks, and a pair of large sea boots cost 1 riksdaler and 2 marks. As mentioned earlier, Strøm estimated that there were 500 sea boats with crews of 6 men per boat—which would have meant 3,000 men and 11,000 riksdaler to buy leather outfits for all of them. Leather clothes lasted a maximum of three years, and each year the leather needed repair, which cost around 500 riksdaler for 3,000 men. When you add this sum to the total amount, you get 11,500 riksdaler, which, according to Strøm, made for an annual expense of 3,833 riksdaler and 2 marks.[76] Leather clothes also had to be oiled to keep them soft, with a mixture of cod-liver oil, melted tallow, and a little tar. Leather hats had to be oiled with cod-liver oil, too; a well-oiled leather hat could last twenty years, and therefore was a good investment.

The Old Norwegian sheep is an old breed of Spelsau raised by fisher-farmers. Today it is also called the *Steinaldersau* ("Stone-Age") or *Utegangersau* ("outdoor") sheep. Photo: Ragnhild Stette.

Spelsau Sheep in the Starring Role

Sheep were the main source of raw materials for fishermen's clothing, setting aside the materials for the leather outfit. Wool was absolutely indispensable for men who had to go out to fish. It was important to have the right type of wool for all undergarments, and especially for sea mittens and outer garments made with *vadmal*. Fisher-farmers raised Gammelnorsk sheep, a type of Spelsau with a larger variation in wool characteristics, colors, and horn size and shape than the modern Spelsau. This sheep type has been referred to by several names; for the sake of simplicity, we'll use the word "Spelsau" in this book when we refer to this older type of sheep. Spelsau colors can vary from almost white and gray to brown and black in various shades. Their wool fleece has two types of fiber—one is the long, stiff, strong outer hair coat, and the other is a shorter, softer undercoat with a lot of lanolin. The fibers are lofty, with lots of space for trapped air, which provides insulation and holds in body warmth. Wool adjusts to moisture in the environment by absorbing moisture from damp air, but emitting moisture in dry air. When wool absorbs water, it emits warmth, whereas it consumes warmth as it dries out. This is why wool is so good for clothing in cold and damp weather, and we still use it today because there's no better substitute. Wool can hold up to 35 percent of its weight in moisture without feeling wet, which was wonderful for fishermen. Fleeces were carefully sorted in order to exploit wool's qualities to the maximum. The soft undercoat was used for clothing such as collars, breast cloths, and wrist warmers to protect the skin at sea. The long outer coat was excellent for weaving *vadmal* cloth for sweaters, because its fibers repel water while at the same time holding in warmth. Outercoat hair from the sheep's back, sides, and halfway down the thighs was used for sea mittens. The garments under the sea sweater were less important, so that wool didn't need to be as carefully chosen as the wool for *vadmal* garments.[77]

Spelsau sheep were not shorn; instead, their fleece was "plucked" (the Shetland term "roo" is often used in English to refer to this method). This technique has many advantages: when wool fibers are not cut to remove them from the sheep, they don't draw moisture in through their cut ends, and the layer of fat coating the outside of the fibers isn't broken. This keeps the wool almost completely water-resistant and very durable, making it excellent for textiles that are constantly exposed to moisture. Spelsau were rooed at the beginning of May; the wool had to be "harvested" before a new wool coat began to grow out, which would make the old wool fall away. Wool could be gently pulled off in small staples, or rolled off in large sections from the body of the sheep. The outer coat was separated from the undercoat before carding, and youngsters and servant girls had the job of carding the soft wool into rolags (short rolled tubes of wool fiber ready for spinning). The outer coat was combed with coarse wool combs and drawn out into thin slivers, which were wound around the hand, ready for spinning. These coarse wool combs were used in Iceland, Shetland, and the Faroe islands.[78]

Petter Dass wrote about the lifestyle of the Spelsau and the resources people could gather from these sheep, and he honored the animal as follows:

> The most glorious Røst can be praised from
> Grass-covered Rocks that Nature has given them,
> Where Sheep thrive so well;
> There they run wild every Winter and Spring,
> And are not rescued by men,
> Nor ever given a handful.
> Yet these Beasts bear excellent Wool,
> And are on the Body, so full of Fat,
> That their flesh is rather Fat-round;
> In Winter they wander with the Wool in the Snow,
> So lovely, so pure, so delightful to see,
> That scarcely more beautiful can be found.
> When the Year courses round to Holy Cross Day,
> People on the land must use Diligence to
> Pluck the fully grown Wool;
> But if it is neglected, then the Sheep
> Undress themselves on their Backs and Thighs,
> Until they can become free.
> There the Strangers that usually there row,
> Well, many times found a heap or two
> Of Clothing that what the Sheep lose;
> Nature has given the Beast,
> In Winter they will supply their Skin,
> And in Spring they scrape off their Fleece.[79]

In the nineteenth century, county governors wanted a new standard set for wool; in fact, they wanted a softer and more even wool than Spelsau wool. New types of sheep were developed, such as Dalasau, Rygja, and Steigar, crossbred from Spelsau and English breeds. These are the Norwegian sheep we are familiar with today. They are all included under the general category of Norwegian white sheep. These new sheep breeds became popular; they produced double the amount of wool as the old Spelsau, although better wool led to worse leather.[80] The yield from these sheep was reported very differently to local county governors—men in some districts estimated an average of about 8 marks, while men in other places estimated only 2-3 marks.[81] A sheep cost 1-2 spesidaler; for comparison, a cow cost 8-18 spesidaler, and a horse, 10-50 spesidaler.[82] These new sheep breeds had to be clipped with shears, and the sheep were usually shorn every spring and fall. In northern Norway, they were shorn three times a year because the people who lived there thought it made them produce more wool.

The clipped wool should, as much as possible, hang together as a fleece, so it was rolled together into a wool bundle. This wool bundle could supposedly be used to test a girl to find out whether she would be a good wife. The girl had to throw the wool fleece she had clipped over the house roof; if it came apart, she was ill-suited to being a farm woman.[83]

Processing raw material from sheep into finished wool products involved hard and extensive labor. To begin with, a farm-wife would have bred and fed the sheep she tended, with all the care, tears, and worries that entailed. What should she do, if, for various reasons, she lost a sheep? Before shearing, a sheep has to be washed. After shearing, wool has to be carded on a variety of carders to blend the wool fibers so they can be spun and then plied into yarn. Spinning wheels came to Norway in the first half of the seventeenth century. Before that, women and children spun with hand spindles, the oldest tools for spinning thread. In the period of hand spindles, yarn was spun the same way people later knitted—it happened whenever there was "spare" time. Strong yarn had to be plied with several single strands, and was usually wound into skeins or balls after it was washed. One informant told Kjellmo that people in Lofoten used fish bile to wash newly-spun yarn, in order to make it especially white.[84] Finished yarn was used to knit or to weave fabric. After fabric was cut from a loom, it had to be stomped on and pressed to make it shrink and turn it into firm, thick *vadmal*. Originally, cloth was laid in a large tub of warm water and stamped with bare feet; later on, people had stamping mills with water-driven hammers to perform this heavy work. When wool fabric was woven for sea sweaters, it was important to set up a wide enough weave to avoid any need to seam the pieces. The fabric was then stamped and shrunk to make it strong enough to stand up on its own. With that, fishermen could stay dry even in torrential rain. Fabric and yarn could also be dyed, but for everyday wear, natural sheep's colors were used, and the best sea sweaters were made with undyed wool. If there were too few black sheep, there might be nothing to work with but white wool. At the same time, some textiles were very colorful—for that, women collected and processed plants, leaves, and lichen for dyeing. Of course, dyeing was also work, and required both resources and time to accomplish.

To make extra strong garments, goat hair was blended with sheep's wool. *Vavottene* mittens (see page 38) that were particularly exposed to damage and wear often had goat hair in the yarn. *Ragg* yarn—a term for long, coarse, tangled yarn, usually made of goat hair—was also used for over-stockings called *ragg* stockings. Goatskin was also used for fishermen's leather outfits; but one informant from Vesterålen with whom Trætteberg spoke maintained that goat skin was not often used because goats were "intolerable as domestic animals." Despite the informant's experience, goatskin was definitely used in leather outfits in Vesterålen. Other types of animal hair were used for *vavottene* and over-stockings to strengthen them. Human hair and horse tail hair had the same qualities as goat *ragg* when twisted. Sheep's wool was spun separately, and then horse tail hair was knitted together with the resulting wool yarn. Mittens made with this yarn didn't shrink the way pure wool mittens did, and they didn't absorb moisture. The same applied to cow's hair. Dog and fox hair could also be spun together with sheep's wool for *vavottene*. Whalers would have had mittens knitted with women's hair and wool, and it was said that there were no mittens warmer than these.[85]

Imports and Fashion Trends

Norway imported both clothing and fashions for fishing outfits. However, functionality was considered more important than style. Some garments were more influenced by fashion trends than others, but trends were mostly confined to undergarments. Function determined shape and the way each garment was made, for both knitted and leather clothing. Folk fashion was a concept introduced by the Swedish ethnologist Håkan Liby. Folk costume was the farmers' traditional everyday wear, a style that was the counterpart to the fashion typical for the middle class and bureaucratic officials. Farmers wanted to follow fashion, but they lacked the means to do so and they weren't well-informed about the latest trends. Thus, country fashion ended up somewhere in between traditional folk costumes and the stylish contemporary clothing worn in larger towns. We can tell what was an element of folk fashion and what was a stylish costume based on fashion trends. We can discern geographical differences in folk costume between regions and villages, but fashionable clothing is more distinctly differentiated by period. Folk costumes are timeless; they belonged to the common

Fisherman wearing an "Icelander" and sou'wester, photographed in 1908.
Photo: Anders Beer Wilse (1865-1949). Owner: Norsk Folkemuseum.

people, and were local. Fashionable clothing was worn by the higher social classes, was international, and looks and styles changed much more quickly. For Norway, the clothing of the upper class was the ideal, and thus that of the European royal houses, but most people didn't have the means to meet such standards. They settled for trying to copy the cut and materials to the best of their ability. Liby described these semi-stylish folk fashions as "the meeting between the traditional forms of production in the home and bourgeois fashion innovations, interpreted by local tailors." This led to a characteristic style that took on a life of its own in farming communities, distanced from the fashion ideals of the time. At the same time, elements were borrowed from it.

During periods of economic prosperity, it was easier for farmers to refresh their wardrobes and bring themselves closer to compliance with upper-class fashion; conversely, during bad times, they had to keep wearing older, outdated clothing for multiple years in a row. The garments that combined to form a fisherman's leather outfit didn't have the same age when it came to their cut. Leather skirts are cut in a way that parallels cuts used in prehistoric times—the main cut is a type of primary cut that has survived through the ages because it was appropriate and time-tested. Hans Strøm wrote in 1762: "The Wolf-skirt or Wool dress that was worn by Harald Haarfagres Gigants, the well-known Berserker, had, without a doubt, the same shaping that we have for the useful Leather skirt."[86] This is a reference to Harald Hårfagres, also known as Harald I Fairhair, the first king of Norway, who is said to have died in 930; Strøm assumed his clothing would have had a similar cut, though without discussing why he thought that. Fishermen's leather pants have a newer cut, but nevertheless, their wide, skirt-like legs retain a style recognizable since Viking times. Overall, the leather outfit kept the same shaping over a very long time because it had proven so suitable for its use, and there was no better substitute or other material that outcompeted leather. Garments such as hats and boots do have certain elements taken from fashionable garments; Hans Strøm wrote in 1762 that leather hats have the same shape as "common hats but were not upturned."[87] Trætteberg thought that Strøm was speaking here about pointed hats from the Rococo period (approximately 1720-1785) when he referred to common hats, and that means that fishermen's leather work hats incorporated style trends, at least to some degree. Return to Table IV on page 20 and look at figure 4 to see a man wearing one of these pointed hats with upturned edges. It isn't known when earlier brimmed hats came into use for fishermen's outfits.[88] The *vadmal* clothes that fishermen wore underneath their leather outfits were embellished in accordance with folk fashion. At the same time, these garments might have retained an older overall form, because it was practical when fishing. In the same way that a folk costume could be composed of several different styles, fishermen's costumes might likewise.[89]

Norway also imported wool garments from both the European continent and the Atlantic Ocean islands on a large scale. Home production continued at the same time. *Vadmal* is well-known from archaeological finds from the Iron Age, and weaving for *vadmal* was traditional women's work in all the Nordic countries. Sixteenth-century sources detail imports of *vadmal* from Iceland, the Faroe Islands, and Shetland. The fabric was used for mittens, stockings, and sweaters.[90] A century later, in the 1600s, Norway imported large numbers of thick mittens, stockings, and sweaters from Iceland and the Faroe Islands. The traditional pattern motifs for "Icelander" sweaters are well-known and beloved by Norwegians today, and marketed as "authentically Norwegian." Beginning in the middle of the 1700s, these sweaters were imported to Bergen. Trætteberg thinks that the name "Icelander" comes from having been made on Iceland,[91] but Annemor Sundbø suspects that Icelanders originated in the Faroe Islands, and there are no sources stating that they were originally produced in Iceland. Sundbø has written that the export of such sweaters increased from the Faroe Islands at the end of the 1880s and that they were often knitted with Icelandic wool, which might have given rise to the name Icelander. Another explanation for the name could be the English word for an island dweller—"islander," which looks the same as the Norwegian word *Islander* or "Icelander," according to Sundbø. At the same time, similar sweaters were also produced in both Denmark and Sweden.[92]

The red hats worn by Norwegian fishermen along the coast originally came from France. Hans Strøm wrote in 1762 that men were wearing the "Red French caps."[93] Eventually, many of these red hats were imported rather than home-knitted. There were also imported stocking caps from Holland and Germany, in addition to those from France, and this continued throughout the entire nineteenth century. The imported caps were often double-layered, with a white inner cap as a lining. Skippers from northern Norway also brought stocking

Fishermen from the Faroe Islands photographed in 1898, with red stocking caps, white stockings, *vadmal* jackets, striped overshirts, and knitted sweaters striped in gray and white with "lice" spots. Photo: Johannes Klein. Coloring: Julius Jääskeläinen.

caps home from Bergen. In addition to imports from France, Shetland women knitted red hats and mittens that were sold to foreign fishermen, including Norwegians and Dutchmen. Hats with pattern knitting were also a style that came from abroad. Fishermen along the Jutland coast, the North Frisian islands, and Schleswig and Rügen in Germany and Maren in Holland, had similar stocking caps. In the county of Veile in Jutland, multi-colored night caps or stocking caps were common up until the end of the 1700s, when red hats took over. In Norway, the traditional red hats date back further than patterned ones.[94]

It wasn't only wool clothing that was imported for fishermen's outfits. In the 1880s-1890s, large amounts of chamois leather from Switzerland were used for leather outfits. Chamois was softer and tighter than Norwegian goatskin, but it was tanned the same way. This foreign leather could be purchased from traders in Kvaløy at Torghatten. As far as undergarments went, after 1850, Norwegian fishermen wore work blouses (*busserull*), a common European work garment. Finally, it's also said that Norway exported knitted garments. In 1628, hundreds of Norwegian stockings were sent to Holland and Friesland with lumber that the Dutch picked up in Norway every year.[95] A lively trade between fishermen and traders of various countries circulated knitted garments across borders, and fishermen's wives could examine foreign designs and find new inspiration for exciting motifs and color use in the garments they themselves knitted.

Faroe Island fishermen on the way home from fishing off Iceland in 1898. Here we can see single-color knitted sweaters in blue and green, and one with dark blue, brown, and white stripes. Photo: Johannes Klein. Coloring: Julius Jääskeläinen.

The Fisherman's Outfit in the North Sea Area

The fisherman's outfit, from innermost layer to outermost, is similar all along the Norwegian coast, with only a few local variations. Therefore, it's necessary to look outside Norway's borders to discover whether there are alternatives to the traditional Norwegian fisherman's outfit. In her work, Trætteberg researched Iceland, the Faroe Islands (Denmark) and Shetland (Scotland) in the North Sea area. Fishing around these islands had the same challenges in an open boat. Each of these areas was inhabited or settled by Norwegians at various points, and this common history may have influenced fishermen's outfits in these places. Continued contact was evident via imports and the exchange of textiles. Trætteberg found out that, even if there were many common trends, the differences were larger. The raw materials used were the same—leather and sheep's wool—but the islanders used skins from different animals than Norwegians. Chemical elements and tanning methods also varied, for making leather outfits. Raw tanned skin is watertight, but water can penetrate the seams, and that is where differences lay. The placement of seams and cut of the garment were different in each of the three countries Trætteberg examined.[96] It's important to note that this information applies to the leather outfit only, as this was the main focus of Trætteberg's research. Wool undergarments and inner garments were primarily made the same way in all four places. There were, of course, frequent exchanges of knitted garments for fishing, where fishermen bought pullovers, mittens, hats, and stockings from each other. If a fisherman didn't have a leather outfit, outer *vadmal* clothing was worn as a substitute. This was common in Norway, Iceland, and the Faroe Islands. Trætteberg also thought it was likely that Norwegian leather pants were of the same type as North European trousers from the sixteenth century. She didn't delve into trousers worn in the Mediterranean Sea area, but nevertheless she was able to find out that Norwegian fishermen's clothing belonged to a type worn all along the continental Atlantic seacoast of Europe, from Portugal in the Iberian south up to Finnmark, in the far north of Norway. She was not able to follow the outfit continuously, but found persistent similarities.[97]

The traditional leather outfit was worn for a longer time in Iceland than in Norway, and in some areas it was used all the way up to 1930. Icelanders had three variants of the leather skirt, made with hides from sheep, calves, or horses. Leather pants were made of sheep, buck, calf or horse skin, and went down over the feet to cover the soles. Icelandic fishermen wore sea shoes, which they pulled on over their trousers, to cover their legs. These were made of cowhide or knitted with horsetail yarn. A sou'wester was a common head covering, and white wool sea mittens were used also, with two thumbs on each mitten. Underneath the leather outfit, Icelandic fishermen wore many layers of wool clothing, as in Norway. The undershirt was white *vadmal* but it was replaced by knitted under-sweaters around 1900. The underpants were knitted, as general rule, but also could have been made of *vadmal*. Icelandic fishermen wore knitted pullovers on top of their undershirts, with an extra pullover when it was cold. It was normal to wear a knitted under-sweater, a *vadmal* shirt over the under-sweater, and a knitted pullover over everything else. The outer pants were *vadmal*, and up to the middle of the nineteenth century, these pants reached down to the knees, as in Norway. Icelandic fishermen also wore two pairs of wool stockings, plus under-socks, which went to the lower part of the calf, and over-stockings, which went up over the knees. When trouser legs became longer, men wore only the shorter socks for an inner layer, combined with long sea stockings that went up over the thighs, pulled on over the pants. Other knitted garments included a knitted hat, wrist warmers, and scarf, as in Norway. Icelandic scarves were made with high-quality, soft wool in natural sheep's colors, and often had lengthwise stripes. The hats were either stocking caps or round and tight fitting.[98]

Faroese fishermen also wore leather outfits as late as 1920, even if most of them had switched to oilcloth. Aside from that, a Faroese fisherman had traditional equipment that was neither as warm nor as tight as those of Norwegians and Icelanders. Faroese fishermen wore leather shirts made of lamb's or sheep's skin that was pulled on over the head. Their pants went down to their ankles, and were made of skin from old sheep, which was considered to be strongest against damage. They also wore sheepskin leather strips around their wrists, which were later replaced by knitted wrist warmers like those we've already discussed from Norway. Faroese fishermen wore black hoods, either knitted or *vadmal*, and sea mittens knitted with white or gray wool, with either one or two thumbs. On their legs, they wore brown or gray inner stockings that went up to the knees, with low over-stockings of the same color, reaching under the ankles. Some wore low sea shoes made of knitted wool, with felt or *vadmal* soles, which actually didn't keep water out. Others wore leather shoes made from cow, horse, or seal skin. Under their leather outfits, Faroese fishermen wore two or three white *vadmal* wool shirts that went down to the middle of the thigh. In earlier times, they didn't wear underpants because their long undershirts were sufficient. In severe cold, they protected their sexual organs with a bag-shaped wool holster. This item was also used in Norwegian villages. These were replaced eventually by white *vadmal* trousers, which were later replaced in their turn by knitted underpants. Faroese fishermen also wore colorful knitted pullovers, and scarves knitted with natural gray or white sheep's wool. These scarves were folded to double them lengthwise.[99]

In Shetland, fishermen had already begun to set aside the traditional leather outfits by 1822, although they were still worn in some areas. In general, however, fishermen in Shetland switched over to a fisherman's jacket and trousers. Their leather outfits were made of tanned sheepskin, and consisted of an over-garment with sleeves, pulled on over the head and reaching down to the knees, plus short, wide leather pants. Their sea boots, wide and knee-high, were made of leather from cattle. The edges of their pant legs went over the boot shafts. They covered their heads with hats similar to English or Scottish night caps, in vivid colors that could be seen from a long distance away.[100] Trætteberg's sources didn't say anything in particular about clothes worn underneath these outer garments, or about knitted garments such as pullovers, stockings, and mittens, but it's a given that these were also worn in Shetland.

New Times

The traditional fisherman's outfit was eventually replaced by garments that were cheaper and more easily available, thanks to new materials. This also led to more modern styling. At the end of the nineteenth century, leather was replaced by oilcloth, and some woolen items were replaced by cotton equivalents. Most importantly, these clothes were no longer made at home, but bought at a shop. Outer garments such as leather skirts or *vadmal* sea jackets were exchanged for jackets made of sailcloth, oilcloth, plastic, or rubber. The same considerations also applied to trousers; pants of leather or sailcloth were now made of oilcloth, rubber, or plastic. Footwear made of oiled leather was replaced by rubber footwear. Trætteberg wrote that in villages in northern Norway, a change was made in leather trousers around 1880. The front piece on traditional trousers was lengthened so that it reached up over the chest, an area that came to be called the *bukskinn* in Norwegian, and was held in place by straps over the shoulders—rather like overalls, or pants with suspenders. During the second half of the nineteenth century, oilskins came into use, complete with *bukskinn*. It's unclear whether the leather pant *bukskinn* was surpassed by oilskin pants, or the other way around, according to Trætteberg.[101]

Wool was still important for use in undergarments because of its ability to absorb moisture, a quality lacking in cotton. Nevertheless, cotton became popular, blended with wool, for overshirts and work blouses at the end of the nineteenth century. Undershirts that had once been made entirely out of wool were, by the 1870s, woven with cotton warp and wool weft. These shirts went straight down to the middle of the thighs. Overshirts were also made this way in northern Norway, around the same time.[102] The traditional leather hat, with a knitted cap underneath, was still in use by the 1850s, but after that, sou'westers became common all along the coast. A drawing by Wilhelm I. Bergstrøm in 1840 shows fishermen wearing oilskin sou'westers on the coast outside Bergen. In Lofoten, men wore regular leather hats with a felt lining until after 1900. Both *våsehatter* and traditional leather hats had features found in the sou'westers that followed them, which were made with oilskin. During the 1860s, the leather in *våsehatter* was replaced by oilskin, and the crown was joined in points, as for a sou'wester. In northern Norway, the term "sea hat" was still used for a sou'wester in the 1960s, but it was more common to call it a sou'wester.[103]

The name is basically the same everywhere sou'westers were worn: southwester in England and *südwester* in Germany.

Leather sleeves were replaced by oilskin, but these new sleeves had the same shaping as traditional leather sleeves. Oilskin sleeves were sewn by fishermen's wives, and fishermen prepared them with linseed oil. Fishermen still wore half-sleeves in the 1960s, but by then they were made of plastic. Today, polyamide is used, as well as other synthetics.[104] Sometime around 1900, leather aprons were replaced by oilskin aprons. In the 1860s, factories producing oilskin outfits for fishermen were founded in cities such as Stavanger, Ålesund, Fredrikstad, Haugesund, Moss, and Kristiania (present-day Oslo). Some of these factories specialized in rubber clothing, while others used linseed oil to impregnate the fabric. Oilskin outfits were made with linseed oil.

Despite these new and modern materials, parts of the old outfits were still used. Oral traditions about the use of leather pants were still passed along in northern Norway by the 1950s, when Trætteberg was pursuing her research. She was told that most continued to use leather pants for sea fishing through the 1870s. Men in the far north continued to wear leather pants long after leather skirts had been replaced by oilskins, and it was the same in Hordaland. It was said that leather pants were the most important garment in the traditional leather outfit, and the lingering widespread use of them supports that assertion. Well-oiled leather trousers lasted 3, 4, or sometimes even 5 years, which was twice as long as oilskin pants. Informants also related that, when motor-driven boats appeared around 1900, leather pants were still part of sea-fishing outfits. Tanner K. Frøslie in Tromsø said the following in 1961: "As late as 1905-06, I remember that the Bodø tanners had a mass of calf skins to process. The skins had been sent in by people in Saltnes and the North Helgeland districts, with orders that the skins should be used for leather trousers."[105] Even in 1958, there were still a handful of fishermen in leather trousers in Balsfjord, even if plastic and rubber were more common.

Newer types of boats also became available, and leather

outfits generally disappeared from use at the same time that motor and deck boats took over. The same happened with boat ryas. During the 1880s, *åttring* boats were left behind both technologically and economically by deck boats. It also became more difficult to find enough crewmen for open boats. The small fishing smacks that replaced these open boats had nice, cozy enclosed decks, and were much more secure and more comfortable for fishermen to work on. They could also take in a larger catch. During the winter fishing in 1886, for example, four small smacks from Løvsøya caught a total of 44,200 cod—11,000 cod per boat.[106] However, even if deck boats were becoming more popular, there were still fishermen who continued to fish in open boats, wear leather outfits, and use boat ryas.

Today, working fishermen follow the guidance of the Norwegian Maritime Directorate when it comes to clothing for fishing in extreme cold:

> **Clothing for Cold Conditions**
> One should choose underclothes that absorb and transport sweat away from the body at the same time that they insulate. Layers of clothing should insulate and draw sweat further away (breathe). Outer clothing should protect against environmental conditions and reduce moisture levels inside clothing. Footwear should have shoe soles with friction to counteract slipping, but also be airy and insulating. Safety helmets, gloves, eyeglasses, and hearing aids must function in the cold. If normal clothes do not provide sufficient protection against cold, the employer must have the necessary extra clothing at hand. Such clothing is considered personal protective gear and the cost should be assumed by the employer.[107]

The fishermen's outfit has changed since fisher-farmers went out to fish in open boats, but the weather and the need to protect the body against the elements is the same. The Norwegian Maritime Directorate says nothing about the materials this clothing should be made of, only the characteristics it should have, and they are the same for undergarments, in-between clothing, and outer clothing as they were for the traditional garments fishermen wore in the eighteenth to twentieth centuries. These characteristics have been equally important for 250 years; the knowledge of many generations, gained through trial and error, led to a fishing outfit that hasn't functionally changed in several centuries. The traditional Norwegian fishing outfit has a standardized style precisely because the people who made it had found a formula that worked, and no one was able to improve on it until the twentieth century.

KNITTING PATTERNS

Read through the entire pattern before you begin knitting! Also, make sure your knitting gauge matches the gauge given in the pattern instructions. Work a swatch, measure it, and adjust your needle size as necessary.

Abbreviations and Terms

BO	bind off (= UK cast-off)
CC	contrast or pattern color
cm	centimeters
CO	cast on
est	established
in	inch(es)
k	knit
m	meters
MC	main or background color
mm	millimeters
p	purl
pm	place marker
rep	repeat
rnd(s)	round(s)
st(s)	stitch(es)
RS	right side
tbl	through back loop(s)
tog	together
WS	wrong side
yo	yarnover

felting /fulling — Techniques that use similar processes to make wool firmer and more durable. These processes include repeated stamping or pounding of wool in soapy water, usually alternating between warm and cold water. Felting begins with wool fiber; fulling is worked with woven or knitted wool fabric.

Icelander — A pullover sweater knitted in the Faroe Islands for export. They usually had a white background with pattern motifs in dark brown and sometimes red from lichen dyes.

steek — A section of extra stitches added so you can knit in the round on a sweater body that will later be cut open for the two fronts of a cardigan or for the armholes from underarms to shoulders, or for the neck (for example, a placket). Usually the steek stitches are worked in alternating pattern colors or with one color for single-color rounds. Instructions for reinforcing and cutting a steek are given in individual patterns.

vadmal — A firm wool fabric made from woven cloth (usually tabby or twill) that has been heavily fulled by pounding and/or stomping on the woven piece in warm soapy water.

He looked out on the rough Sea;
It would be unpleasant to go out there;
But Fish played down in the deep Waters,
And that Play he wanted to see.

Ivar Aasen, "Millom bakker og berg" [Between Hills and Mountains], third verse.

RECONSTRUCTION VS. INSPIRATION

Clothing reconstruction can be achieved by using several different sources, such as preserved clothes—original models, as they might be called—and photographs, drawings, paintings, or written or oral sources. The patterns in this book were inspired by historic written descriptions, paintings, and photographs. Preserved clothing is the foremost primary source used, especially when it is in good condition. This makes it possible to carefully assess the material, cut, and techniques, and gain firsthand knowledge of the garment we want to recreate. The challenge lies in ascertaining whether the extant garment is representative of the type to be reconstructed. A textile collection at a museum, for example, does not necessarily capture a true picture of the reality of the past or the ways people were actually clothed, unless a thorough and professional effort has been undertaken. Museum collections are sometimes formed by more passive methods: members of the public donate items, which are then included in museum collections. In that case, the resulting collection may be a random assortment of items donors thought were important, pretty, or simply old enough that they ought to be taken to a museum. It can be a challenge to locate enough examples of one type of garment to be able to reasonably claim that there was a costume tradition at work, not just the taste and style of a single person. Recycling and re-sewing was common all over Norway, which means past features of one style may have been reshaped to look more like another, making it difficult to identify garments of the same kind. All around Norway as well as in Europe, museum collections have primarily housed and preserved elegant garments; few everyday outfits were collected in comparison to finer clothing, which was typically upper-class. In addition, there is the phenomenon of folk fashion to consider. People re-made and recycled due to economic circumstances, and old clothes were used for all kinds of purposes—for example, they may have been cut up and used for filling in bedding, insulation in buildings, or to make boat ryas and floor rugs. It was common to use up everyday clothes in every possible way, until they couldn't be used for anything else, and certainly weren't in any shape to be given to a museum. It was different with fine clothing, especially regarding smaller articles of clothing; it wasn't possible to re-work them, and they didn't require much space to keep packed away. People often believe that only fine, well-maintained items should go to museums, and so museum collections have gaps in their collections of everyday textiles. When it comes to everyday household items, museum collections tend to be more comprehensive.

Very important secondary sources, when it comes to the reconstruction of traditional clothing, are watercolors and drawings. The ethnologist and researcher Aagot Noss (1924-2015) wrote several books about this subject. By the nineteenth century, particularly in connection with efforts to build a national identity, many artists traveled around and studied, recorded, and drew Norwegian nature, history, buildings, and folk life. These artists drew various scenes with men and women on farms, clothed in their Sunday best or festive outfits. National romanticism foregrounded folklife and folk costume as major motifs in art. However, not all artists were equally reliable as historical sources. They might have taken artistic liberties, borrowed, copied, or plagiarized each other. In many instances, costume watercolors and drawings that various artists made of the same clothes were very much alike—potentially evidence of *artistic borrowing*. Clothing and costume traditions were also described in written and oral sources. The drawback with these is that sometimes the source could not be corroborated afterwards, as it was not connected to concrete items but was a reminiscence, or was something an informant had heard secondhand from older individuals who were no longer around. Such sources might not have worn that type of clothing themselves, but had been told about it or had seen it as a child. It's important to be especially critical about these sources, but if they agree overall with other materials, they can reinforce or confirm our understanding of traditional styles of dress.

There are a good number of preserved leather outfits

around Norway—perhaps because it was valuable equipment that meant life or death for fishermen, and it was costly and time-consuming to make. Leather outfits took space to preserve when they were no longer used, but luckily they weren't all discarded or recycled. The situation is worse for common knitted garments that would have been worn at other times besides out at sea. At the Sunnmøre Museum, unfortunately, there are few examples of important garments such as sweaters, hats, and sea mittens, especially compared to the number and scope of what must once have existed. Sea mittens were exposed to wear and tear to the highest degree, and were typically "used up." Other knitted garments that survived fishing could be worn every day. The threshold was also high for giving a pair of well-worn long underpants, with holes and patches, to a museum. But when enough sources are gathered, we come to a point that results in the garments that actually are found in Sunnmøre Museum. The clothes are few, but descriptions and pictures show that they follow a tradition that was common to all of Norway. These garments are part of the material we used as inspiration for the knitting patterns in this book. We made the definitive choice not to *reconstruct* garments, but to let ourselves be *inspired* by them. We wanted to create living, modern, wearable garments, and reconstruction would have placed major limits on that project. Reconstruction means an exact copy of clothing that already exists, and takes away the opportunity to play with colors and patterns—opportunities we know were taken all the time, when wives knitted garments for their fishermen. We hope our readers will choose colors and motifs that the wearer or knitter likes, so the garments they make will be worn often. A reconstruction also includes finding or making materials as close as possible to the originals. Yarn can be expensive to recreate, because techniques for yarn production are different today than they were 150 to 200 years ago. It should be easy to get yarn that can be used, but today there are far fewer of us who produce yarn the same way our foremothers did. The quality of modern yarn may also be different from "historically correct" yarn; we feel it's important that a garment be worn, rather than lying folded away in a drawer because it's scratchy or itchy.

Reconstruction can also be a dynamic process, because in the eighteenth and nineteenth centuries, garments were fitted to the body that wore them. So reconstructions must also fit today's wearers—you can't push someone into garments that simply don't fit well, but the cut and techniques have to be historically accurate. When it comes to leather outfits, it would be impossible to copy any given piece of clothing precisely, because skins will always be different sizes from garment to garment. Again, it's the cut and technique that are important.

Photo: Kristin Støylen.

BRASS BUTTONS

Brass buttons were the equivalent of silver for folk costume, because they were cheaper than buttons, pins, or other embellishments made of more expensive metal. Hand-molded buttons like these were common all around Norway; in fact, these are copies from folk costumes in the Sunnmøre Museum. According to Eilert Sundt, buttons were held aside from service pay in the first half of the nineteenth century, which indicates that buttons were costly items. We would like for there to be a new use for these pretty brass buttons, which are most often used today for folk costumes. So we used them for the sweaters in this book that have buttons.

VIKING BANK

"Sawtooth"-patterned cardigan
—a design from Salhus Tricotagefabrik

SKILL LEVEL

Intermediate to Experienced

SIZES

S (M, L, XL)

The sample shown in the photos is knitted in size L.

FINISHED MEASUREMENTS

Chest: as measured at underarms, 37 (38¼, 47¼, 48½) in / 94 (97, 120, 123) cm

Total Length: 26 (26¾, 27½, 28¼) in / 66 (68, 70, 72) cm

Sleeve Length: from wrist to underarm, 20 (21, 21¾, 22½) in / 51 (53, 55, 57) cm

MATERIALS

Yarn:

CYCA #3 (DK, light worsted) Hillesvåg Tinde Pelsullgarn (100% Norwegian wool, 284 yd/260 m / 100 g)

Yarn Colors and Amounts:

Natural White 3: 250 (250, 300, 300) g

Olive Green 2118: 550 (550, 600, 600) g

Needles: U. S. sizes 4 and 7 / 3.5 and 4.5 mm: circulars and sets of 5 dpn

Notions: 8 buttons of size desired

GAUGE

24 sts and 26 rnds in stockinette pattern on larger needles = 4 x 4 in / 10 x 10 cm.

Adjust needle size to obtain correct gauge if necessary.

BODY

With smaller circular and Olive Green, CO 255 (263, 271, 279) sts. Work back and forth in k1, p1 ribbing for 2¾ in / 7 cm. Change to larger circular and begin charted pattern; *at the same time*, increase 10 sts evenly spaced across first row = 265 (273, 281, 289) sts. At the end of the row, CO 5 sts for steek (see page 60) at center front. Join and pm

VIKING BANK

"Sawtooth"-patterned cardigan — a design from Salhus Tricotagefabrik

for beginning of rnd and at each side. Make sure pattern is centered, and begins and ends with same pattern stitch, to ensure it is symmetrical.

Work in pattern until body measures 15¾ in / 40 cm (all sizes). When piece measures 22½ (23¾, 24¾, 26) in / 57 (60, 63, 66) cm, or desired length, shape neck: BO 5 steek sts at center front. On each side of neck, BO 11-3-2-2-1-1 sts = 225 (233, 241, 249) sts rem. Place all rem sts on a holder.

SLEEVES

With smaller dpn and Olive Green, CO 48 (52, 56, 60) sts. Divide sts onto dpn and join; pm for beginning of rnd.. Work around in k1, p1 ribbing for 2¾ in / 7 cm. Change to larger dpn. Knit 1 rnd, increasing 8 sts evenly spaced around. Center pattern on sleeve.

Shape Sleeve: On every 5th rnd, increase 1 st at beginning and end of rnd, 3 times. Now increase on every 6th rnd until there are 96 (100, 104, 108) sts. At desired length, knit 1 rnd with Olive Green and then purl 5 rnds for facing. BO loosely.

Make second sleeve the same way.

FINISHING

Machine-stitch 2 lines on each side of center steek stitch.

Measure width of top of sleeve and then measure that length down from shoulder at side of body. Pin at point for base of armhole. Machine-stitch 2-3 zigzag lines on each side of center armhole stitch. Gently steam press sweater before attaching sleeve to make it easier to place pieces edge to edge. Carefully cut armholes open up center st and then attach sleeves by hand. Sew sleeve top facing down over cut edges.

Join shoulders with mattress or Kitchener st. Depending on how many sts were used for setting in sleeves, the number of sts may vary slightly.

NECKBAND

With smaller circular and Olive Green, pick up and knit sts around neckline, including held neck sts. Make sure the total is an odd number of sts. Work back and forth in k1, p1 ribbing for 2¾ in / 7 cm. BO in ribbing. Fold neckband in half and sew down on WS.

FRONT BANDS

The buttonhole band is traditionally the left front band for men and the right front band for women.
With smaller circular and Olive Green, pick up and knit an odd number of sts along front edge and neckband (3 sts for every 4 rows). Work back and forth in k1, p1 ribbing.

Buttonhole Band:
Work 4 rows in ribbing.

Next Row: Space buttonholes about 17 sts apart.
Buttonhole: BO 2 sts and, on next row, CO 2 sts over each gap. After buttonholes, work 4 more rows in ribbing. BO in ribbing, making sure edge is not too tight.

Button Band: Pick up and knit same number of sts as for opposite band. Work 10 rows in k1, p1 ribbing. Finish as for other band.

Weave in all ends neatly on WS.

Sew on buttons. Our version of this sweater has hand-molded brass buttons from Sunnmøre Museum.

FRØYA BANK

White pullover with patterning
in black and green

SKILL LEVEL
Intermediate to Experienced

SIZES
S (M, L, XL)
The sample shown in the photos is knitted in size XL.

FINISHED MEASUREMENTS
Chest: as measured at underarms, 57½ (58¼, 59, 59¾) in / 146 (148, 150, 152) cm
Total Length: 24½ (25¼, 26, 26¾) in / 62 (64, 66, 68) cm
Sleeve Length: from wrist to underarm, 18¼ (19, 19¾, 20½) in / 46 (48, 50, 52) cm

MATERIALS
Yarn:
CYCA #2 (sport, baby) Rauma Finull PT2 (100% Norwegian wool, 191 yd/175 m / 50 g)
Yarn Colors and Amounts:
White 0401: 350 (350, 400, 400) g
Black 0410: 50 (50, 100, 100) g
Green 4018: 50 (50, 100, 100) g
Needles: U. S. size 2.5 / 3 mm: 16 and 32 in / 40 and 80 cm circulars and set of 5 dpn

GAUGE
23 sts and 30 rnds in stockinette = 4 x 4 in / 10 x 10 cm.
Adjust needle size to obtain correct gauge if necessary.

BODY
With long circular and White, CO 240 (260, 280, 300) sts. Join, being careful not to twist cast-on row; pm for beginning of rnd. Work around in k2tbl, p2 ribbing for 1½ in / 4 cm. After completing ribbing, work in stockinette, and *at the same time*, on Rnd 1, increase 20 sts evenly spaced around = 260 (280, 300, 320) sts. Pm at side = 130 (140,

150, 160) sts each for front and back. Knit 10 rnds with White before beginning charted pattern.

NOTE: There are 18 rnds in White between each pattern panel.

Work around in charted pattern up to neckline. Size XL has 5 pattern panels + 10 rnds White.

Shape Neck: Begin working back and forth as you shape neck: Place 20 sts of center front on a holder = 55 (60, 65, 70) sts rem on front for each shoulder. On each side of front neck, BO or decrease 1 st 2 times.

Place 24 sts of center back on a holder = 53 (58, 63, 68) sts rem for each shoulder.

SLEEVES

With dpn and White, CO 36 (40, 44, 48) sts. Divide sts onto 4 dpn and join; pm for beginning of rnd (center of underarm). Work around in k2tbl, p2 ribbing for 1½ in / 4 cm. After completing ribbing, work in stockinette, and *at the same time*, on Rnd 1, increase 12 sts evenly spaced around = 48 (52, 56, 60) sts. Knit 10 rnds with White before beginning charted pattern; *at the same time*, begin shaping sleeve (see below). Count out from center of sleeve to determine stitch for beginning pattern so it will be symmetrical on sleeve.

Shape Sleeve: Increase 1 st on each side of first st every ⅝ in / 1.5 cm until there are 86 (94, 102, 110) sts and you've worked almost to desired length to underarm. Finish with 16 rnds in White.

Make second sleeve the same way.

FINISHING

Join shoulders with mattress or Kitchener stitch. Depending on how many sts were used for setting in sleeves, the number of sts may vary slightly.

Measure width of top of sleeve and then measure that length down from shoulder at side of body. Pin at point for base of armhole. Machine-stitch 2-3 zigzag lines on each side of center armhole stitch. Gently steam press sweater before attaching sleeve to make it easier to place pieces edge to edge. Carefully cut armholes open up center st and then attach sleeves by hand.

NECKBAND

Place the 20 front and 24 back neck sts on short circular, and *at the same time* pick up and knit 22 sts on each side of neck = 88 sts total. Work around in k2tbl, p2 ribbing for 2 in / 5 cm. Fold band in half and sew down on WS.

Weave in all ends neatly on WS.

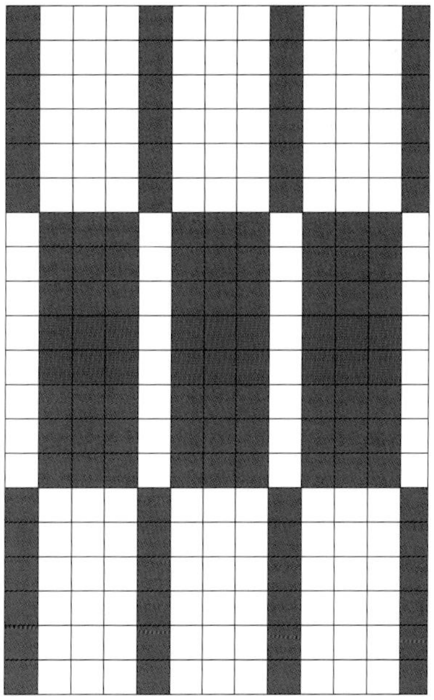

SKLINNA BANK

Hat with pattern panel

SKLINNA BANK

Hat with pattern panel

SKILL LEVEL

Intermediate

SIZES

M (L, XL)

FINISHED MEASUREMENTS

Circumference: 19¾ (20, 20½) in / 50 (51, 52) cm

Length: 9½ (9¾, 10¼) in / 24 (25,26) cm

MATERIALS

Yarn:

CYCA #2 (sport, baby) Rauma Finull PT2 (100% Norwegian wool, 191 yd/175 m / 50 g)

Yarn Colors and Amounts:

Black 0410: 100 (100, 100) g

White 0401: 50 (50, 50) g

Green 4018: 50 (50, 50) g

Needles: U. S. size 2.5 / 3 mm: 24 in / 60 cm circular and set of 5 dpn

Notions: 4 stitch markers

GAUGE

22 sts and 28 rnds in stockinette = 4 x 4 in / 10 x 10 cm.

Adjust needle size to obtain correct gauge if necessary. With circular and Black, CO 112 (116, 120) sts. Join and pm for beginning of rnd. Work around in k2tbl, p2 ribbing for 1½ in / 4 cm, or desired length of brim. Change to stockinette, increasing 4 sts evenly spaced on first rnd. Knit 5 rnds with Black and then begin charted pattern. When cap is 6¼ (6¾, 7) in / 16 (17, 18) cm long, begin shaping crown with Black. Pm with 29 (30, 31) sts between each marker. Change to dpn when sts no longer fit around circular.

On *every other* rnd, decrease on each side of each marker = 8 sts decreased, until 72 (80, 84) sts rem. Now decrease the same way on every rnd until 24 (28, 32) sts rem. Cut yarn and draw end through rem sts; tighten. Weave in all ends neatly on WS.

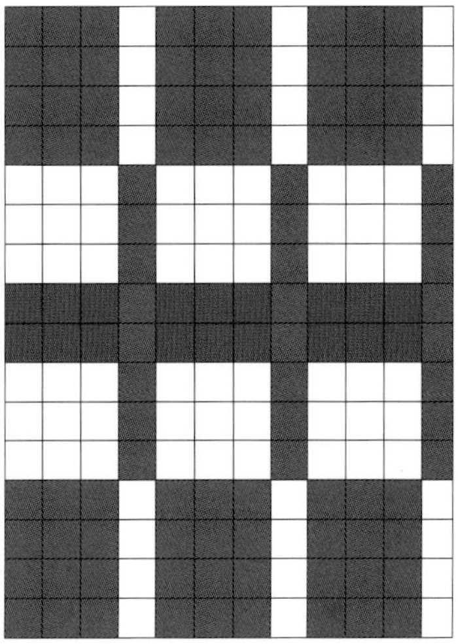

HALTEN BANK

Under-sweater with neck placket

SKILL LEVEL

Intermediate

SIZES

S (M, L, XL)

The sample shown in the photos is knitted in size XL.

FINISHED MEASUREMENTS

Chest: as measured at underarms, 48¾ (49¾, 50½, 51¼) in / 124 (126, 128, 130) cm

Total Length: 26¾ (27½, 28¼, 29¼) in / 68 (70, 72, 74) cm

Sleeve Length: from wrist to underarm, 18¼ (19, 19¾, 20½) in / 46 (48, 50, 52) cm

MATERIALS

Yarn:

CYCA #3 (DK, light worsted) Sandnes Merinoull (100% Merino wool, 114 yd/104 m / 50 g)

Yarn Colors and Amounts:

Blue-Gray 6071: 600 (600, 650, 650) g

Light Blue 6531: 50 (50, 50, 50) g

Putty 1015: 50 (50, 50, 50) g

Rust 4035: 50 (50, 50, 50) g

Brown 2564: 50 (50, 50, 50) g

Needles: U. S. size 4 / 3.5 mm: 16 and 32 in / 40 and 80 cm circulars and set of 5 dpn

Notions: 3 buttons of size desired

GAUGE

20 sts and 30 rnds in stockinette = 4 x 4 in / 10 x 10 cm. Adjust needle size to obtain correct gauge if necessary.

HALTEN BANK

Under-sweater with neck placket

BODY

With long circular and Blue-Gray, CO 250 (260, 270, 280) sts. Join, being careful not to twist cast-on row; pm for beginning of rnd. Work around in k1tbl, p1 ribbing for 2½ in / 6 cm. Change to Light Blue and knit around until yarn runs out (about 2¾ in / 7 cm). Knit stockinette bands of the same width in Putty, Rust, and then Brown. Continue with Blue-Gray until body measures 18¼ (19, 19¾, 20½) in / 46 (48, 50, 52) cm. Now you are at the underarms.

Divide body for back and front with 125 (130, 135, 140) sts for each. Work back and front separately.

Back: Work back and forth in stockinette to shoulders, 11¾ (12¼, 12¾, 13) in / 30 (31, 32, 33) cm (same length as width of sleeve top).

Front: Work back and forth in stockinette for 2½ (2¾, 3¼, 3½) in / 6 (7, 8, 9) cm or desired length for neck placket: divide front in two with 62 (65, 67, 70) st for each half (BO center st on sizes S and L). Work each side separately. On first row, CO 7 sts for each placket band. Work each band, beginning on center front edge, as: Sl 1 purlwise wyf, (k1, p1) 3 times. This makes a smooth chain edge.

On left side of placket, make a total of 3 2-st buttonholes: Work in ribbing for 1½ in / 4 cm. Work 2 sts on band, BO 2 sts, work rem 3 sts of row; turn. Sl 1, rib 2 sts; turn to RS and CO 2 sts (knit-CO). Turn to WS and finish row. Space rem 2 buttonholes evenly up band.

When front is 8¾ (9, 9½, 9¾) in / 22 (23, 24, 25) cm long, place the 7 band sts plus 3 extra sts on a holder and shape neckline: BO 1 st once, 2 sts 7 times. Rem sts are for shoulder. Join shoulders with mattress or Kitchener stitch. Depending on how many sts were used for setting in sleeves, the number of sts might vary slightly.

SLEEVES

With Blue-Gray and dpn, CO 36 (40, 44, 48) sts. Divide sts onto dpn and join. Work around in in k1tbl, p1 ribbing for 1½ in / 4 cm. Work around in stockinette, increasing 12 sts evenly spaced around on first rnd = 48 (52, 56, 60) sts. Every ⅝ in / 1.5 cm, increase 1 st on each side of 1st st (center of underarm) until there are 98 (102, 106, 110) sts. BO loosely. Make second sleeve the same way.

NECKBAND

Place held front neck sts onto circular. Pick up and knit 8-9 sts on each side of neck and also place held back neck sts on circular. Join and work around in k1tbl, p1 ribbing for ¾ in / 2 cm. BO firmly (but not too tightly).

FINISHING

Attach sleeves by hand. Sew on buttons. Our version of this sweater has hand-molded brass buttons from Sunnmøre Museum.

Weave in all ends neatly on WS.

SHETLAND BANKS

Long pants with cord tie at waist

SKILL LEVEL
Intermediate

SIZES
S (M, L, XL)
The sample shown in the photos is knitted in size L. These pants are stretchy and flexible because they are ribbed.

FINISHED MEASUREMENTS
Waist: circumference when stretched, 41 (41¾, 42½, 43¼) in / 104 (106, 108, 110) cm; when unstretched, 22 (22¾, 23¾, 24½) in / 56 (58, 60, 62) cm
Total Length: from waist to ankle, 43¼ (45¼, 47¼, 49¼) in / 110 (115, 120, 125) cm
Leg: from crotch to ankle, 31 (31½, 32, 32¼) in / 79 (80, 81, 82) cm

MATERIALS
Yarn:
CYCA #3 (DK, light worsted) Sandnes Merinoull (100% Merino wool, 114 yd/104 m / 50 g)
Yarn Colors and Amounts:
Blue-Gray 6071: 500 (550, 600, 650) g
Needles: U. S. size 4 / 3.5 mm: 16 and 32 in / 40 and 80 cm circulars and set of 5 dpn
Notions: Knitting mill for tie-cord (optional)

GAUGE
32 sts and 28 rnds in k1, p1 ribbing = 4 x 4 in / 10 x 10 cm. Adjust needle size to obtain correct gauge if necessary.

The pants are worked on a circular needle from the waist down, with an eyelet round for the waist tie-cord.

SHETLAND BANKS

Long pants with cord tie at waist

With long circular, CO 154 (168, 182, 196) sts. Join, being careful not to twist cast-on row; pm for beginning of rnd. Work around in k1, p1 ribbing for ⅜ in / 1 cm.

Now make eyelets for tie: (K2, p2tog, yo) around.
Next Rnd: Purl each yarnover.
Suggestions for increases: The suggestions for increases depend on size being knitted. Pm at center front and center back
Sizes S and L: Increase on each side of 3 knit sts at center front and center back.
Increase 1 st by picking up a st of previous rnd and knitting it.
Sizes M and XL: Increase on each side of 2 knit sts at center front and center back.
Increase 1 st by picking up a st of previous rnd and knitting it.
Suggestions for decreases on legs:
Decrease on each side of marker. Before marker, k2tog. After marker: Sl 1, k1, psso.

When piece measures 4¼ in / 11 cm. raise back with short rows:
Work 10 sts past marker at center back; turn. Sl 1 (to avoid a hole) and then work 10 sts past marker on other side; turn. ★Sl 1 and work 10 sts past previous turn★; rep ★ to ★ until there are 14 (28, 22, 16) sts at center front. Turn once more so you will be on RS. Continue around in ribbing on all sts. When piece measures 5½ (5½, 6, 6) in / 14 (14, 15, 15) cm at center front and 8 (8, 8¼, 8¾) in / 20 (20, 21, 22) cm at center back, increase on both back and front: Increase 2 sts at front and back on every 5th (6th, 6th, 7th) rnd, a total of 7 times = 182 (196, 210, 224) sts.
When piece measures 12¼ (13, 13, 13¼) in / 31 (33, 33, 35) cm at center front, BO the first 6 (6, 7, 7) sts, place 79 (85, 91, 97) sts on a holder (= leg), leave next 12 (14, 14, 16) sts on needle for gusset. Place 79 (85, 91, 97) sts on a holder (= leg) and BO rem 6 (6, 7, 7) sts. Work back and forth in stockinette over the 12 (14, 14, 16) gusset sts for 4 (4¼, 4¾, 5¼) in / 10 (11, 12, 13) cm and then sew gusset to the 12 (14, 14, 16) sts you bound off at center back.

LEGS

Place the held 79 (85, 91, 97) sts of one leg onto short circular. Pick up and knit 20 (20, 22, 24) sts along one side of gusset = 99 (105, 113, 121) sts. Pm on inside of leg (that is, at center of the sts you picked up along gusset). Work around in ribbing until leg is 3¼ in / 8 cm long, decrease 1 st at each side of marker.
Shape Leg: Decrease every 1⅜ (1⅛, 1, 1) in / 3.5 (3, 2.5, 2.5) cm a total of 20 (22, 25, 28) times until 59 (61, 63, 65) sts rem. Change to dpn when sts no longer fit around circular. Continue until leg measures approx. 31 (31½, 32, 32¼) in / 79 (80, 81, 82) cm or desired length. BO in ribbing with knit over knit and purl over purl.
Make second leg the same way by placing sts on second holder onto circular.
Tie Cord: Make a 4-st cord of desired length on a knitting mill, or work I-cord on dpn.
I-cord: CO 4 sts onto 1 dpn. K4. ★Slide sts to front of needle, bring yarn behind needle, tug yarn and k4★; rep ★ to ★ until cord is desired length. Cut yarn and draw end through sts and tighten.
Thread cord through eyelet rnd.
Weave in all ends neatly on WS.

TRÆNA BANK

Cabled pullover with raglan shaping

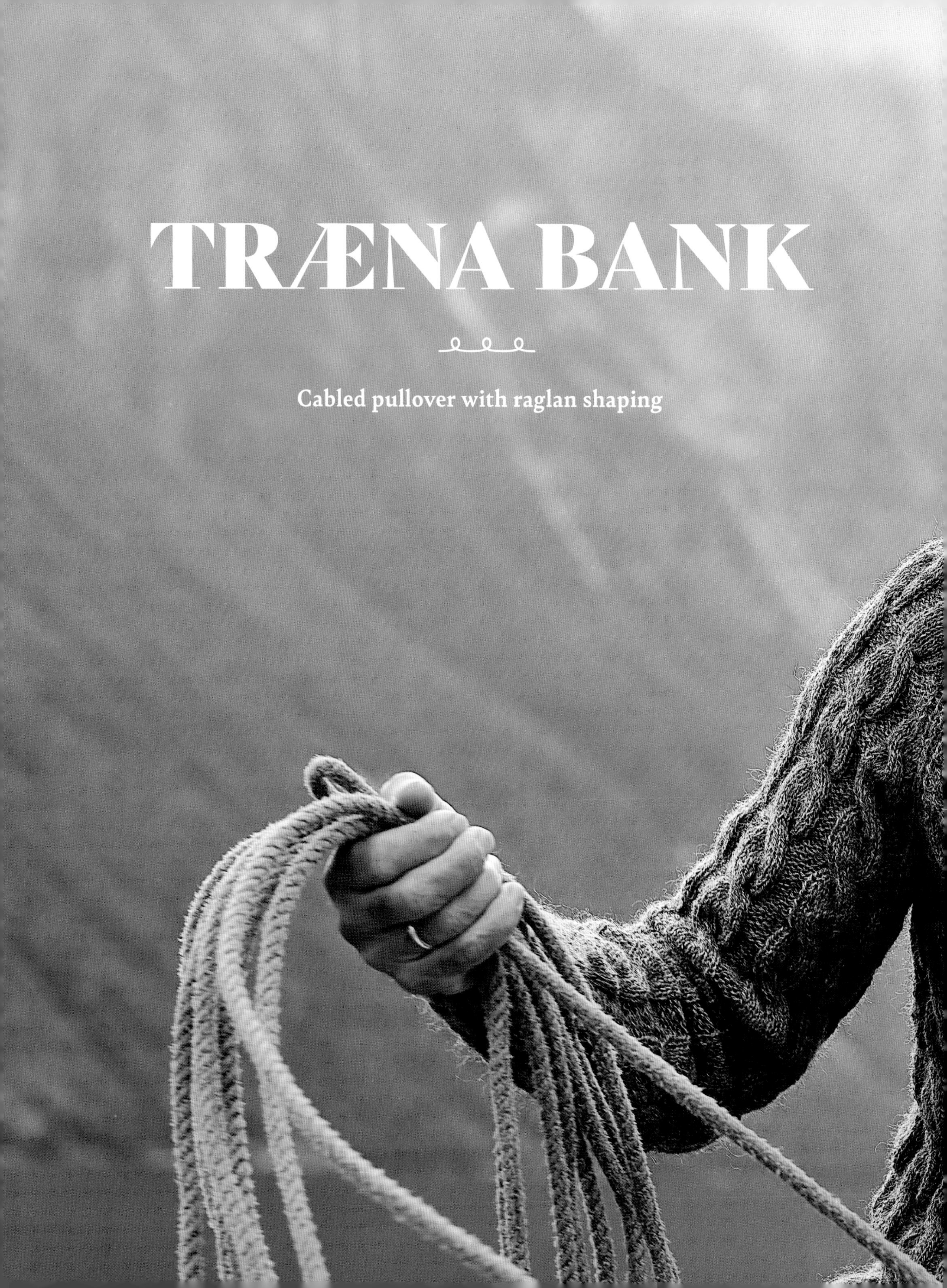

SKILL LEVEL

Intermediate to Experienced

SIZES

S (M, L, XL)

The sample shown in the photos is knitted in size M.

FINISHED MEASUREMENTS

Chest: as measured at underarms, 30¾ (34, 37, 40¼) in / 78 (86, 94, 102) cm

Total Length: 28 (29½, 31, 32¾) in / 71 (75, 79, 83) cm

Sleeve Length: from wrist to underarm, 17¾ (18½, 19¼, 20) in / 45 (47, 49, 51) cm

MATERIALS

Yarn:

CYCA #1 (fingering) Hillesvåg Sølje (100% Norwegian pelt wool, 383 yd/350 m / 100 g)

Yarn Colors and Amounts:

Gray-Blue 2113: 450 (450, 500, 500) g

Needles: U. S. size 2.5 / 3 mm: 16 and 32 in / 40 and 80 cm circulars and set of 5 dpn; cable needle

GAUGE

16 sts and 28 rnds in cable pattern = 4 x 4 in / 10 x 10 cm. Adjust needle size to obtain correct gauge if necessary.

TRÆNA BANK

Cabled pullover with raglan shaping

BODY

With long circular, CO 260 (272, 284, 296) sts. Join, being careful not to twist cast-on row; pm for beginning of rnd. Work around in k1tbl, p1 ribbing for 1¼ in / 3 cm. Knit 1 rnd, increasing 28 sts evenly spaced around = 288 (300, 312, 324) sts.

Cable Pattern

Rnds 1-14: (P4, k8) around.

Rnd 15: (P4, place 4 sts on cable needle and hold in front of work, k4, k4 from cable needle) around.

Continue in cable pattern until body is 15¾ (17¼, 19¾, 20½) in / 40 (44, 50, 52) cm or desired length to underarms. Divide body in two for back and front with 144 (150, 156, 162) sts for each. *At the same time*, BO 10 sts centered at each underarm. Set body aside while you knit sleeves.

SLEEVES

With dpn, CO 40 (52, 64, 76) sts. Divide sts onto 4 dpn and join; pm for beginning of rnd. Work around in k1tbl, p1 ribbing for 1¼ in / 3 cm. Knit 1 rnd, increasing 8 sts evenly spaced around = 48 (60, 72, 84) sts. Work around in cable pattern. *At the same time*, shape sleeve: Every ⅝ in / 1.5 cm, increase 1 st on each side of st at center of underarm until there are 108 (120, 132, 144) sts. Work new sts into cable pattern. When sleeve is approx. 17¾ (18½, 19¼, 20) in / 45 (47, 49, 51) cm long, BO 10 sts centered on underarm.

RAGLAN SHAPING/YOKE

Arrange body and sleeves on long circular = 464 (500, 536, 572) sts. Knit 1 rnd. Pm at each intersection of sleeve and body. The rnd now begins at beginning of back. The raglan lines each consist of 4 sts (2 sts on each side of marker) and are worked as p1, k2, p1.

Decrease Rnd: K2tog before and after the 4 center sts of each raglan stripe.

Knit 1 rnd.

Continue in cable pattern, decreasing as above on every other rnd.

NECK

When body length measures approx. 24½ (26, 27½, 29¼) in / 62 (66, 70, 74) cm or desired length, shape neck. Place 28 sts at center front on a holder and begin working back and forth. *At the same time*, shape neckline: BO 2 sts at neck edge 2 times, 1 st 2 times, while continuing raglan shaping to total length = 28 (29½, 31, 32¾) in / 71 (75, 79, 83) cm.

Neckband

Place held 28 sts onto circular, pick up and knit sts around neck so you have a multiple of 4 and the same number of sts on each side of neck. Work around in k1tbl, p1 ribbing for 1¼ in / 3 cm or to desired length if you want a higher neckband, and then BO in ribbing.

FINISHING

Seam underarms with wool yarn. Weave in all ends neatly on WS.

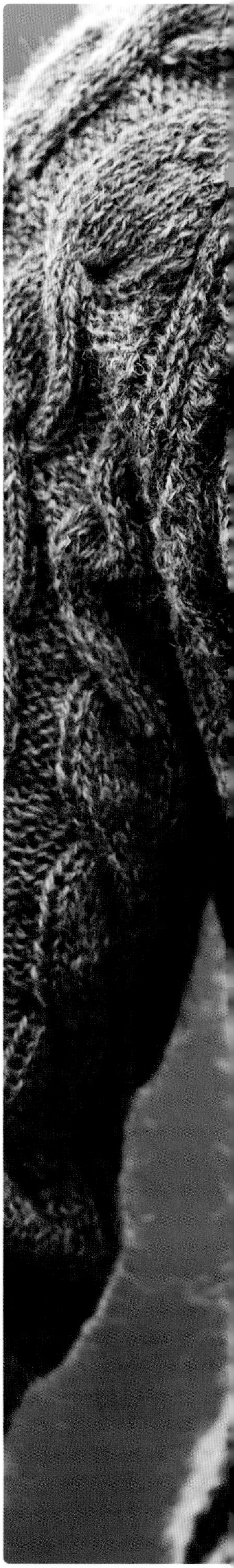

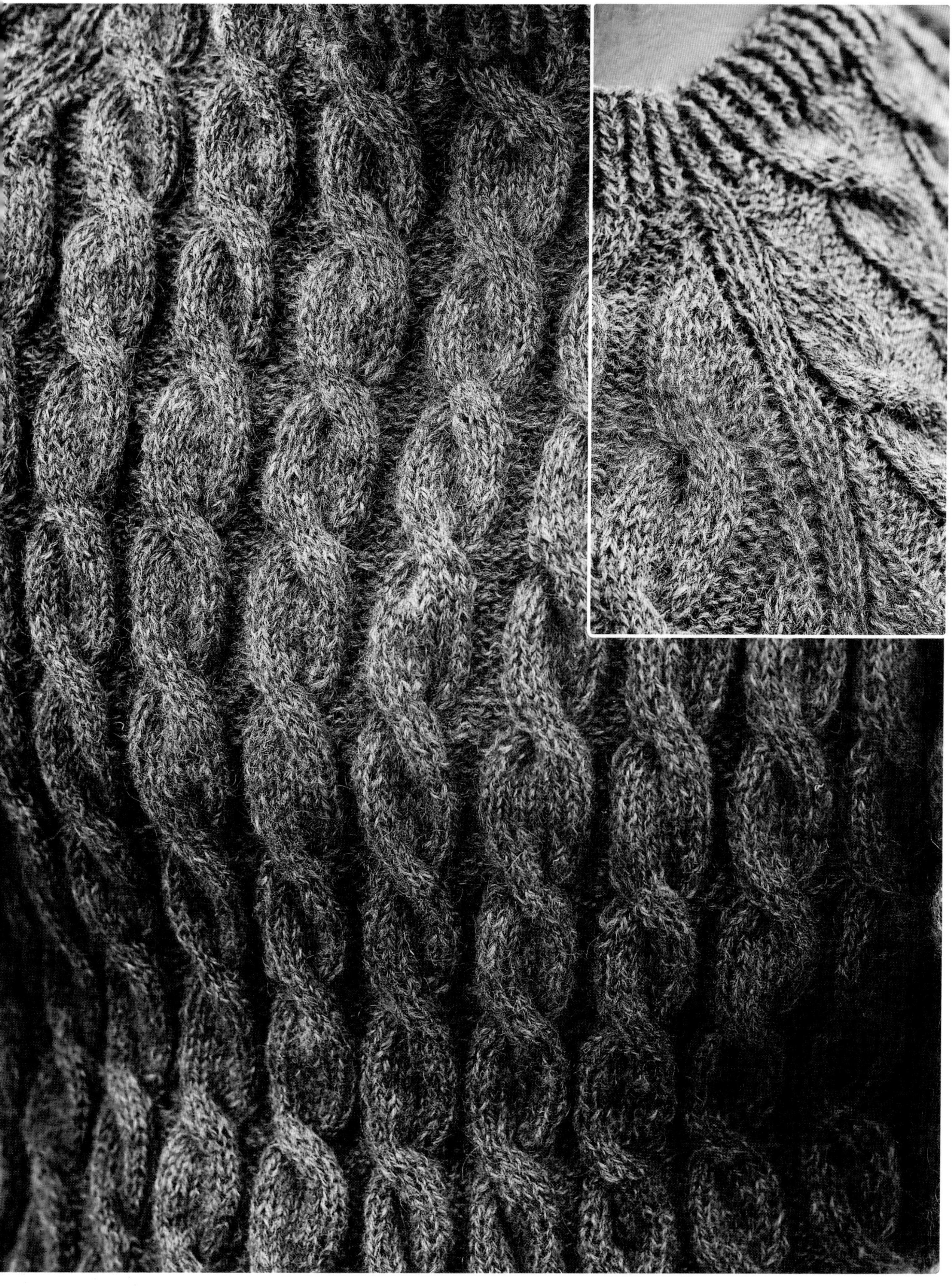

WEST TAMPEN

Lamb's wool under-sweater

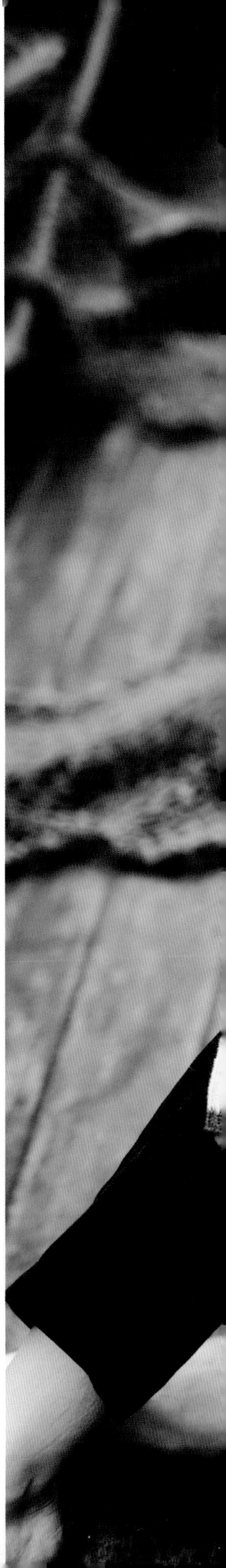

WEST TAMPEN

Lamb's wool under-sweater

SKILL LEVEL

Intermediate

SIZES

S (M, L, XL)

The sample shown in the photos is knitted in size M.

FINISHED MEASUREMENTS

Chest: as measured at underarms, 31 (32¼, 33, 34¼) in / 79 (82, 84, 87) cm

Total Length: 21 (22, 23¼, 24) in / 53 (56, 59, 61) cm

Sleeve Length: from wrist to underarm, 19 (19¾, 20½, 21¼) in / 48 (50, 52, 54) cm

MATERIALS

Yarn:

CYCA #1 (light fingering) Rauma Lamullgarn (100% Norwegian wool, 273 yd/250 m / 50 g)

Yarn Colors and Amounts:

Gray 13: 450 (450, 500, 500) g

Brown 36: 50 (50, 50, 50) g

Mint 23: 50 (50, 50, 50) g

Needles: U. S. size 4 / 3.5 mm: 32 in / 80 cm circular and set of 5 dpn

GAUGE

20 sts and 32 rnds in ribbing = 4 x 4 in / 10 x 10 cm.

Adjust needle size to obtain correct gauge if necessary.

BODY

The back is 3¼ in / 8 cm longer than the front (which you can change if you like).

Front: With circular and Brown, CO 136 (140, 144, 148) sts. Work back and forth in k2, p2 ribbing for 3¼ in / 8 cm. Change to Mint and work 2 rows in ribbing. Change to Gray and continue in ribbing for 1¼ in / 3 cm. Set front aside while you work back.

Back: Work as for front, but make Gray section 3¼ in / 8 cm longer. Now arrange back and front on circular and join to work in the round. Continue with Gray in ribbing until piece measures 11¾ (13, 14¼, 15) in / 30 (33, 36, 38) cm or desired length to underarms.

Divide for Front and Back at Underarms

Divide, with 136 (140, 144, 148) sts each front and back; work each side separately.

Front: Continue in ribbing for 6 in / 15 cm and then shape neck: BO the center 40 sts and work each side separately = 48 (50, 52, 54) sts for each side.

When at total length, BO rem sts in ribbing or place on holder.

Back: Continue in ribbing without neck shaping. When at total length, BO sts in ribbing or place shoulder sts on holder and BO rem sts for back neck.

Join shoulders with mattress or Kitchener st.

SLEEVES

With Brown and dpn, CO 68 (72, 76, 80) sts. Divide sts onto 4 dpn and join; pm for beginning of rnd. Work around in k2, p2 ribbing for 4 rnds. Change to Mint and continue in ribbing for another 4 in / 10 cm. Change to Gray for remainder of sleeve. *At the same time*, shape sleeve: at center of underarm, increase 1 st on each side of first st every ¾ in / 2 cm until there are 110 (114, 118, 122) sts. When sleeve is 19 (19¾, 20½, 21¼) in / 48 (50, 52, 54) cm long, BO loosely in ribbing. Make second sleeve the same way.

FINISHING

Attach sleeves. Weave in all ends neatly on WS.

STOREGGA

Boat neck sweater

SKILL LEVEL

Intermediate to Experienced

SIZES

S (M, L, XL)

The sample shown in the photos is knitted in size M.

FINISHED MEASUREMENTS

Chest: as measured at underarms, 38½ (41¾, 45¾, 48¾) in / 98 (106, 116, 124) cm

Total Length: 23¾ (25¼, 26¾, 28¼) in / 60 (64, 68, 72) cm

Sleeve Length: from wrist to underarm, 20 (20½, 21, 21¼) in / 51 (52, 53, 54) cm

MATERIALS

Yarn:

CYCA #3 (DK, light worsted) Hillesvåg Sol (100% Norwegian lamb's wool, 317 yd/290 m / 100 g)

Yarn Colors and Amounts:

White 400: 500 (500, 600, 600) g

Green 418: 250 (250, 300, 300) g

Needles: U. S. sizes 2.5 and 6 / 3 and 4 mm: 16 and 32 in / 40 and 80 cm circulars and set of 5 dpn (smaller size)

GAUGE

24 sts and 27 rnds in stockinette pattern on larger needles = 4 x 4 in / 10 x 10 cm.

Adjust needle size to obtain correct gauge if necessary.

BODY

With smaller circular and White, CO 228 (234, 240, 246) sts (motifs will not work out evenly around, but mismatches at side seams will be hidden by the arms). Join, being careful not to twist cast-on row; pm for beginning of rnd. Work around in k1, p1 ribbing for 3½ in / 9 cm or desired length (all sizes). Change to larger circular and knit 3 rnds with White. Now work in charted pattern, until body measures 23¾ (25¼, 26¾, 28¼) in / 60 (64, 68, 72) cm or desired length to shoulders.

If possible, end by working "lice" section. Knit 2 rnds with White. Divide body in two with 114 (117, 120, 123) sts each on a needle or holders.

Work each half separately back and forth in k1, p1 ribbing for 4 rnds. Join the outermost 26 (28, 30, 32) sts on each side with mattress or Kitchener st for shoulders. BO rem sts firmly.

SLEEVES

With smaller dpn and White, CO 44 (46, 48, 50) sts. Divide sts onto 4 dpn and join; pm for beginning of rnd. Work around in k1, p1 ribbing for 1¼ in / 3 cm. Knit 1 rnd, increasing 8 sts evenly spaced around = 52 (54, 56, 58) sts. Knit 1 rnd with White and then work in charted pattern. *At the same time,* shape sleeve: at center of underarm, increase 1 st on each side of first st every ⅝ in / 1.5 cm until there are 112 (114, 116, 118) sts. Knit 6 rnds with White and then BO loosely. Set sleeve aside while you make second sleeve the same way

FINISHING

Measure width of top of sleeve and then measure that amount down from shoulder at side of body. Pin at point for base of armhole. Machine-stitch 2-3 zigzag lines on each side of center armhole stitch. Gently steam press sweater before attaching sleeve to make it easier to place pieces edge to edge. Carefully cut armholes open up center st and then attach sleeves by hand.

Weave in all ends neatly on WS.

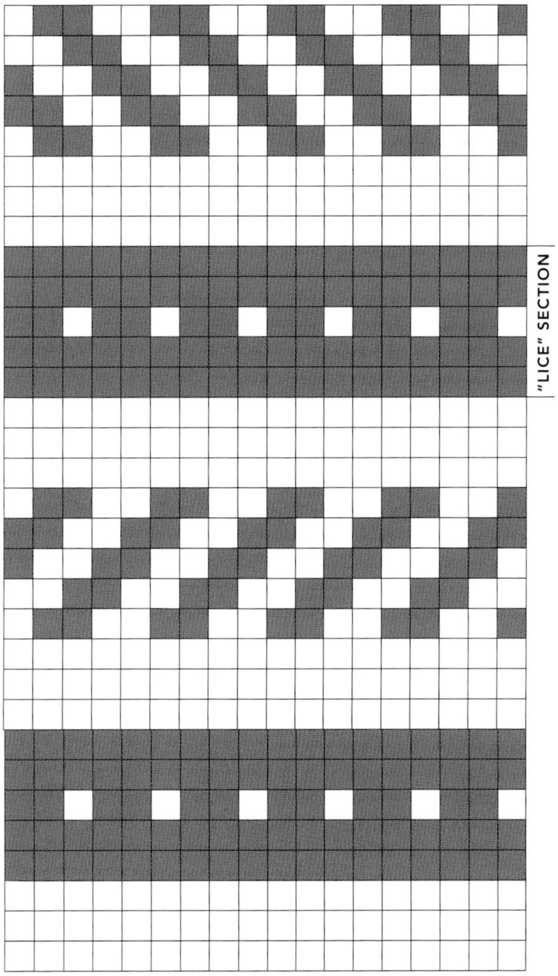

VESTERÅL BANK

Two hats from the same pattern

VESTERÅL BANK

Two hats from the same pattern

FINISHED MEASUREMENTS

Circumference: 19¾ in / 50 cm

Total Length: 9½ in / 24 cm

MATERIALS

Yarn:

CYCA #3 (DK, light worsted) Hillesvåg Sol (100% Norwegian lamb's wool, 317 yd/290 m / 100 g)

Yarn Colors and Amounts:

White 400: 50 g

Green 418: 50 g

Needles: U. S. sizes 4 and 6 / 3.5 and 4 mm: 16 in / 40 cm circular and set of 5 dpn (larger size)

GAUGE

24 sts and 27 rnds in stockinette on larger needles = 4 x 4 in / 10 x 10 cm.

Adjust needle size to obtain correct gauge if necessary.

With smaller circular and MC, CO 110 sts. Join, being careful not to twist cast-on row; pm for beginning of rnd. Work around in k1, p1 ribbing for 3¼ in / 8 cm. Change to larger circular. Knit 1 rnd, increasing 10 sts evenly spaced around = 120 sts. Knit 7 rnds with MC. Now work either step pattern chart between the two 3-st narrow panels. When cap measures 7 in / 18 cm, begin crown shaping.

Crown

NOTE: Change to dpn when sts no longer fit around circular.

Decrease Rnd 1: (K22, k2tog) around = 5 sts decreased.

Decrease Rnd 2: (K21, k2tog) around = 5 sts decreased.

Continue decreasing with 1 less st between decreases on every rnd until 3 sts rem between decreases.

Cut yarn and draw end through rem sts; tighten.

Weave in all ends neatly on WS.

Vesterål Bank with Green MC

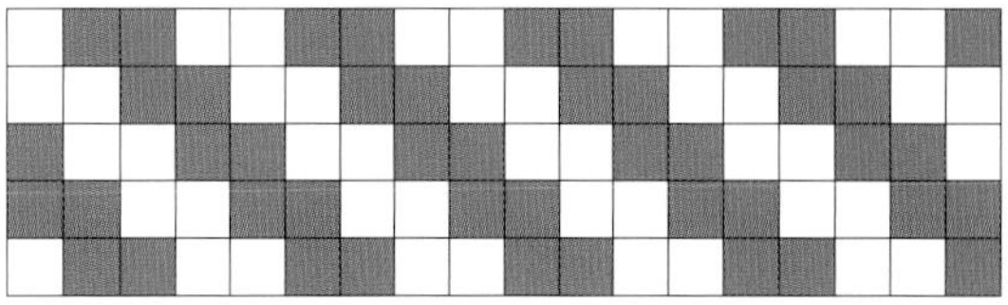

Vesterål Bank with White MC

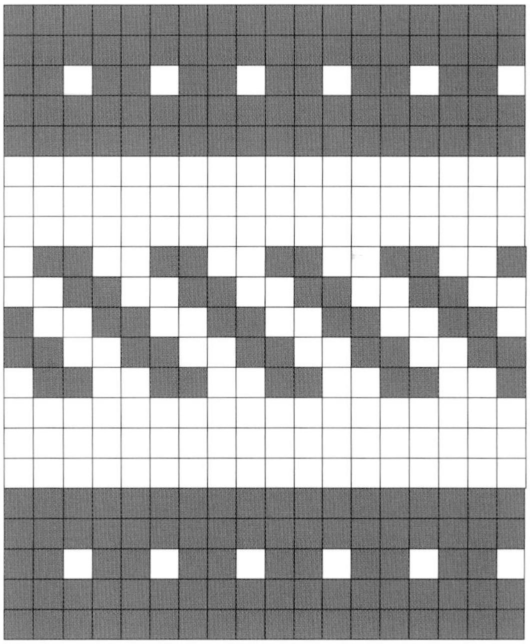

NORTH CAPE BANK

White Icelander in multi-color pattern

SKILL LEVEL

Intermediate to Experienced

SIZES

S (M, L, XL)

The sample shown in the photos is knitted in size XL.

FINISHED MEASUREMENTS

Chest: as measured at underarms, 39½ (43¼, 47¼, 51¼) in / 100 (110, 120, 130) cm

Total Length: 26 (27½, 29¼, 30¾) in / 66 (70, 74, 78) cm

Sleeve Length: from wrist to underarm, 17¼ (18¼, 19, 19¾) in / 44 (46, 48, 50) cm

MATERIALS

Yarn:

CYCA #3 (DK, light worsted) Rauma 3-ply Strikkegarn (100% Norwegian wool, 118 yd/108 m / 50 g)

Yarn Colors and Amounts:

White 100: 600 (650, 700, 750) g

Blue-Black 1387: 50 (50, 50, 100) g

Light Blue 155: 50 (50, 50, 100) g

Blue 167: 50 (50, 50, 50) g

Orange 161: 50 (50, 50, 50) g

Needles: U. S. sizes 4 and 6 / 3.5 and 4 mm: 16 and 32 in / 40 and 80 cm circulars and sets of 5 dpn

GAUGE

20 sts and 24 rnds in stockinette pattern on larger needles = 4 x 4 in / 10 x 10 cm.

Adjust needle size to obtain correct gauge if necessary.

BODY

With smaller circular and White, CO 232 (240, 252, 260) sts. Join, being careful not to twist cast-on row; pm for beginning of rnd. Work around in k2tbl, p2 ribbing for 1½ in / 4 cm. Change to larger circular and knit 3 rnds with White. Work charted pattern until body measures 15 (16½, 18¼, 19¾) in / 38 (42, 46, 50) cm or desired length to underarms. End with 3 rnds of White. BO 16 sts centered at each side. Set body aside while you knit sleeves.

SLEEVES

With smaller dpn and White, CO 36 (40, 44, 48) sts. Divide sts onto 4 dpn and join; pm for beginning of rnd. Work around in k2tbl, p2 ribbing for 1½ in / 4 cm. Change to larger dpn and stockinette pattern. On first rnd, increase 8 sts evenly spaced around = 44 (48, 52, 56) sts. Every ⅝ in / 1.5 cm, increase 1 st on each side of first st (center of underarm) until there are 94 (98, 102, 106) sts. End with 3 rnds of White to match body. BO 16 sts centered on underarm.

Set sleeve aside while you make second sleeve the same way.

RAGLAN YOKE

Arrange body and sleeves on larger circular. Make sure there are 3 rnds of White at top of body and sleeves before you begin pattern knitting. Knit 1 rnd without decreasing, placing a marker at each intersection of body and sleeve. Decrease on every other rnd. Always work decrease st with White. Beginning of rnd is now at beginning of back (pm). On each side of each marker, decrease as follows: ★Knit until 2 sts before marker, k2tog tbl with White, slip marker, k2tog with White★; rep ★ to ★ around. Knit 1 rnd without decreasing and then decrease on following rnd.

NECKLINE

Continue raglan shaping as est until piece measures approx. 23¾ (24½, 26¾, 28¼) in / 60 (62, 68, 72) cm. Now shape neck. Place 30 sts of center front on a holder and begin working back and forth, *at the same time* continuing raglan shaping as est. At neck edge at each side, BO 2 sts at beginning of row once, and then 1 st 2 times. Make sure there are some White sts before you work pattern panel since you will decrease and pick up sts here. When you work pattern on the back, make sure floats stay on WS. Continue with raglan shaping until sweater is total length: 26 (27½, 29¼, 30¾) in / 66 (70, 74, 78) cm. Seam shoulders. Place back neck sts on a holder.

NECKBAND

With smaller circular and White, pick up and knit sts in addition to the held front and back neck sts. Pick up and knit 5 sts on each side of neck shaping. Knit 1 rnd, and *at the same time* decrease 2 sts evenly spaced across front, 2 sts between both raglan decrease lines and 2 sts across back = 8 sts decreased around. Try sweater on and decide if you want a tighter neck. If so, decrease a few more sts evenly spaced around. Make sure you have a multiple of 4 sts before beginning ribbing.

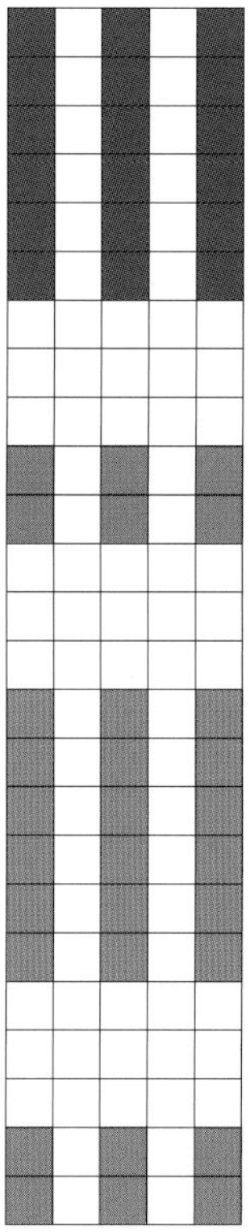

Ribbing: K2tbl, p2 around for ¾ in / 2 cm. BO firmly in ribbing.

Seam underarms with wool yarn. Weave in all ends neatly on WS.

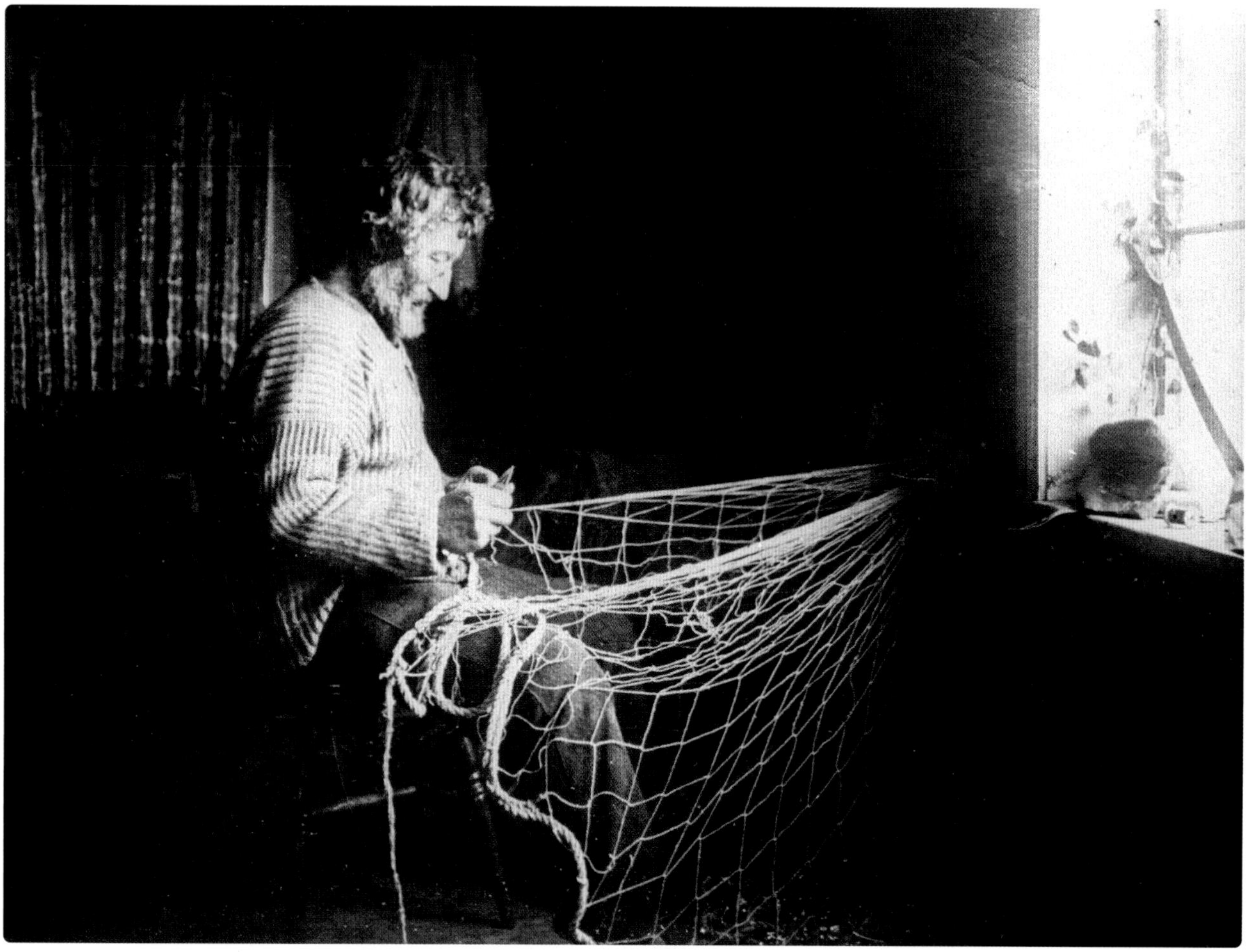

A photo by Berent Martin Henrik Nielsen Schrøder (1845-1900). The light streams in from the window, providing him with light to work. He is wearing a knitted pullover with a pattern of vertical stripes. It's an easy, regular pattern panel and there's a certain calm in the picture. This made me want to repeat the panels in our North Cape sweater. Photo: Schrøder. Sverresborg Trøndelag Folkemuseum.

ROCKALL

Charcoal gray and turquoise pullover
with raglan shaping

SKILL LEVEL

Intermediate to Experienced

SIZES

S (M, L, XL)

The sample shown in the photos is knitted in size XL.

FINISHED MEASUREMENTS

Chest: as measured at underarms, 39½ (41¾, 44, 46½) in / 100 (106, 112, 118) cm

Total Length: 28¼ (29¼, 30, 30¾) in / 72 (74, 76, 78) cm

Sleeve Length: from wrist to underarm, 18¼ (19, 19¾, 20½) in / 46 (48, 50, 52) cm

MATERIALS

Yarn

CYCA #4 (worsted, afghan, Aran) Hillesvåg Embla (Hifa 3) (100% wool, 230 yd/210 m / 100 g)

Yarn Colors and Amounts:

Charcoal Gray 6056: 700 (700, 750, 750) g

Turquoise 6031: 300 (300, 400, 400) g

Needles: U. S. size 6 / 4 mm: 16 and 32 in / 40 and 80 cm circulars and set of 5 dpn

GAUGE

14 sts and 21 rnds in stockinette pattern = 4 x 4 in / 10 x 10 cm.

Adjust needle size to obtain correct gauge if necessary.

ROCKALL

Charcoal gray and turquoise pullover with raglan shaping

BODY

With Charcoal, CO 184 (196, 208, 220) sts. Join, being careful not to twist cast-on row; pm for beginning of rnd. Work around in k2, p2 ribbing for 2¾ in / 7 cm. Knit 1 rnd with Charcoal, *at the same time* increasing 1 (4, 2, 0) sts evenly spaced around = 185 (200, 210, 220) sts, and then begin charted pattern. Work charted pattern until body measures 16½ (17¼, 18¼, 19) in / 42 (44, 46, 48) cm or desired length to underarms. BO 12 sts centered at each side. Set body aside while you knit sleeves.

SLEEVES

With Charcoal, CO 36 (36, 40, 40) sts. Divide sts onto 4 dpn and join; pm or beginning of rnd. Work around in k2, p2 ribbing for 2 in / 5 cm. Knit 1 rnd, increasing 12 sts evenly spaced around = 48 (48, 52, 52) sts. Change to stockinette pattern, counting to center pattern on sleeve. Approx. every ⅝ in / 1.5 cm, increase 1 st on each side of first st (center of underarm), until sleeve is 18¼ (19, 19¾, 20½) in / 46 (48, 50, 52) cm long; BO 12 sts centered on underarm.

Set sleeve aside while you make second sleeve the same way.

RAGLAN YOKE

Arrange body and sleeves on larger circular. Knit 1 rnd without decreasing, placing a marker at each intersection of body and sleeve. The markers are at the center of a 4-st raglan line. Always knit the 2 center sts with Charcoal and 1 st on each side of these with Turquoise. Decrease on every other rnd. Beginning of rnd is now at beginning of back; pm. On each side 4-st raglan stripe, k2tog. Knit 1 rnd without decreasing and then decrease on following rnd. Continue raglan decrease on every other rnd until body measures approx. 25½ (26½, 27¼, 28) in / 65 (67, 69, 71) cm or desired length. Now shape neckline.

NECKLINE

Shape Neck: Place 18 sts of center front on a holder and begin working back and forth, *at the same time* continuing raglan shaping. At neck edge at each side, BO 2 sts at beginning of row 2 times, and then 1 st 1 time.

Continue with raglan shaping until sweater is total length: 28¼ (29¼, 30, 30¾) in / 72 (74, 76, 78) cm. Seam shoulders. Place back neck sts on a holder.

NECKBAND

Pick up and knit sts in addition to the held front and back neck sts. Pick up and knit 7 sts on each side of neck shaping. Make sure you have a multiple of 4 sts before beginning ribbing.

Ribbing: K2, p2 around for 1¼ in / 3 cm or desired length. BO in ribbing.

Seam underarms with wool yarn. Weave in all ends neatly on WS.

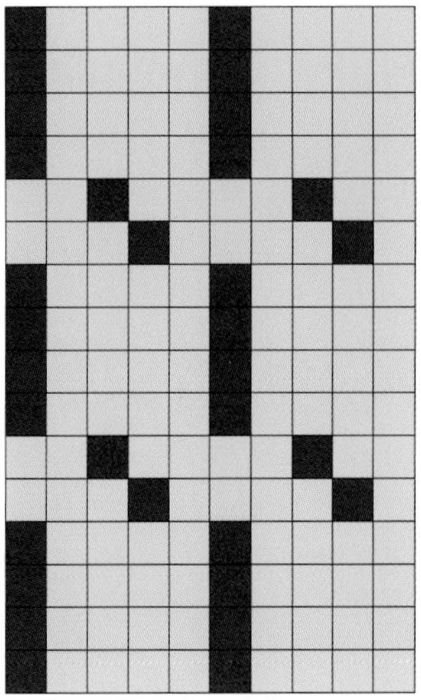

Two photos inspired our Rockall pullover. The photo at the left shows a well-worn Icelander. According to the Kolding Museum, this so-called "Icelander" came from the Faroe Islands. What's especially interesting is that Anders Beer Wilse photographed a man wearing a sweater with the same design. He is standing in a boat, holding a Christmas tree, and talking with three neatly dressed little girls. In an obviously newer photo of a crew in a hatch, two of the men are wearing similar sweaters. It's difficult to say whether these were hand-knitted or factory-knitted. What we can assert is that the pattern motif can be found in a pattern book from the Salhus Tricotagefabrik (Salhus Knitting Factory) from 1909.

Photo: Conni Ramskov, Museum Kolding.

In a newer photo, two of the crew are wearing similar sweaters. Photo: Fosen Bildarkiv (Fosen photo archive) / Bjugn Bygdatunlag.

Fisherman wearing an Icelander and sou'wester, photographed in 1908. Photo: Anders Beer Wilse. Owner: Norsk Folkemuseum.

TROMSØ FLOW

Black zippered jacket

MATERIALS

Yarn:
CYCA #1 (fingering) Hillesvåg Sølje (100% Norwegian pelt wool, 383 yd/350 m / 100 g)
Yarn Colors and Amounts:
Black 2109: 450 (450, 500, 500) g
Red-Yellow 2122: 50 (50, 50, 50) g
Needles: U. S. size 2.5 / 3 mm: 16 and 32 in / 40 and 80 cm circulars and set of 5 dpn
Notions: Separating zipper 21 (24, 25, 27) in / 55 (60, 65, 70) cm long, depending on jacket length

GAUGE

23 sts and 25 rnds in stockinette pattern = 4 x 4 in / 10 x 10 cm.
Adjust needle size to obtain correct gauge if necessary.

This jacket is worked in the round on a circular needle. The center front steek is later cut open. Make sure the zipper and jacket length match.

SKILL LEVEL

Intermediate to Experienced

SIZES

S (M, L, XL)
The sample shown in the photos is knitted in size XL.

FINISHED MEASUREMENTS

Chest: as measured at underarms, 50¾ (51½, 52½, 53½) in / 129 (131, 133, 136) cm
Total Length: 26½ (27¼, 28, 28¾) in / 67 (69, 71, 73) cm
Sleeve Length: from wrist to underarm, 19 (19¾, 20½, 21¼) in / 48 (50, 52, 54) cm

BODY

With long circular and Black, CO 244 (256, 268, 280) sts. Join, being careful not to twist cast-on row; pm for beginning of rnd. Work around in k2tbl, p2 ribbing for 2 in / 5 cm. Knit 1 rnd with Black and then work charted patten. After completing charted rows, continue with Black until body measures 17 (17¾, 18½, 19¼) in / 43 (45, 47, 49) cm or desired length to underarms.
Divide body in two and work back and front separately = 122 (128, 134, 140) sts each for front and back.
Back: Continue back and forth in stockinette until back measures 9 (9½, 9¾, 10¼) in / 23 (24, 25, 26) cm above underarms. Place back sts on a holder while you knit the front.
Front: Continue back and forth in stockinette until front measures 6 (6¼, 6¾, 7) in / 15 (16, 17, 18) cm above

underarms. Place the center 26 sts on a holder and work each side separately. On each side of neck edge, BO 1 st 10 times = 38 (41, 44, 48) sts rem for each shoulder. Place rem sts on a holder.

SLEEVES

With dpn and Black, CO 62 (64, 68, 72) sts. Divide sts onto 4 dpn and join; pm for beginning of rnd. Work around in k2tbl, p2 ribbing for 2 in / 5 cm. Continue in stockinette, increasing 8 sts evenly spaced around on first rnd. Every 1¼ in / 3 cm, increase 1 st on each side of beginning st (center of underarm) until there are 88 (98, 108, 118) sts. When sleeve is 19 (19¾, 20½, 21¼) in / 48 (50, 52, 54) cm long, BO loosely. Make second sleeve the same way.

NECKBAND

Join shoulders with mattress or Kitchener st. There are approx. 44 sts rem for back neck. With Black, pick up and knit approx. 108 sts around neck, including the 44 + 26 held sts. Make sure you have a multiple of 4 sts. Work around in k2tbl, p2 ribbing for 1½ in / 4 cm. Fold neckband in half and sew down edge on WS.

FINISHING

Measure width of top of sleeve and then measure that length down from shoulder at side of body. Pin at point for base of armhole. Machine-stitch 2-3 zigzag lines on each side of center armhole stitch. Gently steam press sweater before attaching sleeve to make it easier to place pieces edge to edge. Carefully cut armholes open up center st and then attach sleeves by hand.

Weave in all ends neatly on WS.

Use a contrast color yarn to hand-baste through center front st from the neck down. Machine-stitch 3 lines on each side of center stitch. Carefully cut front open and remove basting. Sew in zipper.

Important Note: Double-check to make sure jacket length, including neckband, matches zipper length.

They stand there, collected, close together, as if to take off against the wind and weather while they look out over the sea. "Will he round the point?" they wonder, serious, taciturn, staring at the fateful promontory the fisherman is pointing out: A boat they recognize is at the point, struggling to escape the breakers and rocks, to save itself in the shelter on the other side, where the wind must give up its grip.

They are clothed for weather and wind. Wide pants cover their thigh-high boots, leather hats protect their heads and ears, and vests or jackets form an extra layer over their wool sweaters, which are knitted in water-repellant wool from sheep who live outside year-round. There's salt water in the stitches, a warming wool armor against whipping sea and wind. Some houses can be seen in the background; an older man sits with folded hands on a row boat.

The man in the center of the picture is younger than the others. He doesn't have a beard, his face is open, and his look is fixed on the outwards point. He is wearing neither jacket nor vest, but only a patterned fisherman's pullover. A leather hat covers his forehead, and his eyes are focused. He stands bent and tense. Who is out there? Is it a father, a brother, an uncle, a comrade?

This painting, with the younger man in the center of the picture, inspired the garment with this pattern. It became the Tromsø Flow jacket, with the panel around the lower edge imitating the stripes on the man's pullover. Otherwise, the jacket is single-color, worked in black.

Painting by the Danish artist, Michael Peter Ancher (1849-1927): *Will he round the point?*

SPITSBERGEN BANK

Red and white pullover with raglan shaping

SKILL LEVEL

Intermediate to Experienced

SIZES

S (M, L, XL)

The sample shown in the photo is knitted in size M.

FINISHED MEASUREMENTS

Chest: as measured at underarms, 38¼ (41¾, 45¼, 48¾) in / 97 (106, 115, 124) cm

Total Length: 27½ in / 70 cm (all sizes)

Sleeve Length: from wrist to underarm, 17¾ (18¼, 18½, 19) in / 45 (46, 47, 48) cm

MATERIALS

Yarn:

CYCA #3 (DK, light worsted) Rauma 3-ply Strikkegarn (100% Norwegian wool, 118 yd/108 m / 50 g)

Yarn Colors and Amounts:

Copper Red 127: 300 (300, 350, 350) g

Natural White 101: 200 (200, 250, 250) g

Needles: U. S. sizes 4 and 6 / 3.5 and 4 mm: 16 and 32 in / 40 and 80 cm circulars and set of 5 dpn in larger size; 16 in / 40 cm circular in smaller size

GAUGE

18 sts and 24 rnds in stockinette pattern on larger needles = 4 x 4 in / 10 x 10 cm.

Adjust needle size to obtain correct gauge if necessary.

BODY

With larger circular and White, CO 207 (216, 234, 252) sts. Join, being careful not to twist cast-on row; pm for beginning of rnd. Knit around for 1¼-1½ in / 3-4 cm (about 8 rnds).

Eyelet Rnd: *Yo, k2tog*; rep * to * around. Knit 2 rnds.

SPITSBERGEN BANK

Red and white pullover with raglan shaping

Now work from charted pattern, with White as MC on the lower section and Copper as CC. The first 9 sts of the pattern chart are the repeat. Work 3 "branches" of the pattern and then switch colors so Copper is MC and White is CC. Continue in pattern to underarms = 15 (15¾, 16½, 17¼) in / 38 (40, 42, 44) cm or desired length. BO 9 sts centered at each underarm. Set body aside while you knit sleeves.

SLEEVES

With larger dpn and White, CO 36 (45, 54, 63) sts. Divide sts onto 4 dpn and join; pm for beginning of rnd. Knit around for 1¼-1½ in / 3-4 cm (about 8 rnds).

Eyelet Rnd: ★Yo, k2tog★; rep ★ to ★ around. Knit 2 rnds. Work 3 "branches" of the pattern with White MC and Copper CC and then switch colors so Copper is the MC and white is CC. *At the same time*, increase 1 st on each side of center underarm st (first st of rnd). Always knit center st with White.

Now work from charted pattern, with White as MC on the lower section and Copper Red as CC. Increase on every 4th rnd a total of 18 times = 72 (81, 90, 99) sts. Change colors on sleeve as on body. When sleeve is 17¾ (18¼, 18½, 19) in / 45 (46, 47, 48) cm long, BO 9 sts centered on underarm.

Set sleeve aside and make second sleeve the same way.

RAGLAN YOKE

Arrange body and sleeves on larger circular and pm at each intersection of body and sleeve. Knit the 2 sts joining body and sleeve with Copper Red and always work decreases with Copper Red. This makes a red stripe between the raglan decrease lines.

Alternately, you might choose to knit the raglan stripe with the two innermost sts in Copper Red and the two outer sts in White. See the raglan decreases in the Rockall pattern.

Decrease as follows: K2tog before and after the 4 center raglan stripe sts. Knit 1 rnd without decreasing; decrease on next rnd. Continue decreasing on alternate rnds up to neckline.

NECKBAND

Work the neckband with White as MC and Copper Red as CC, using smaller circular. Place the center 9 sts on a holder and work back and forth. Decrease 1 st at each side of neck 6 times, at the same time continuing raglan shaping. With White, pick up and knit sts around neck, including held neck sts. Join and knit 2 rnds with White, and, on first rnd, decrease evenly spaced around to 108 sts (12 repeats).

Begin pattern, aligning it as well as possible with pattern on body. Work 2 branches of pattern (1¼ in / 3 cm) or to desired length. Make an eyelet rnd and then knit 10 rnds with White. BO. Fold neckband at eyelet rnd and sew down edge on WS.

Weave in all ends neatly on WS.

DOGGER BANK

Brioche-knit vest

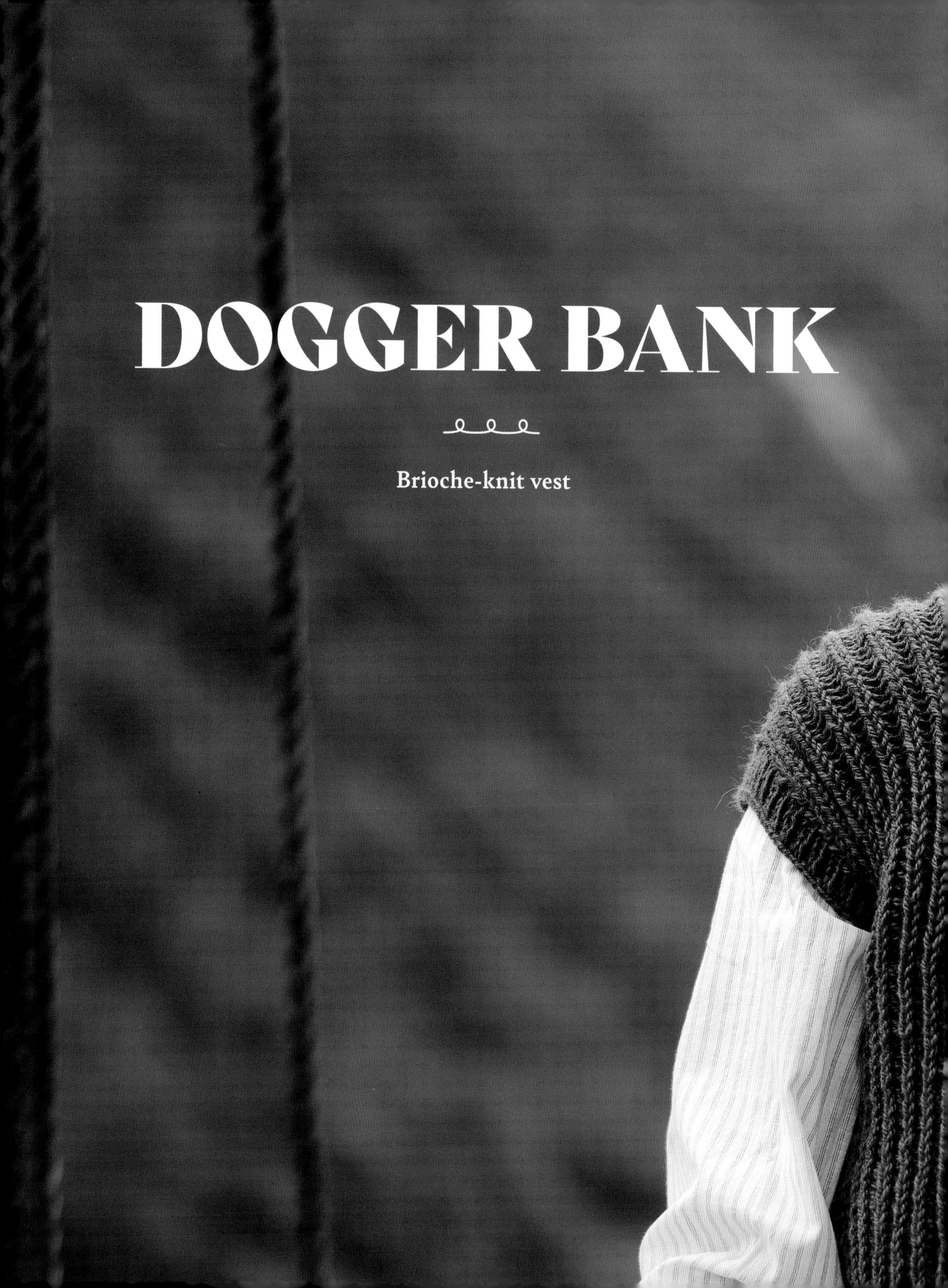

SKILL LEVEL

Intermediate to Experienced

SIZES

S (M, L, XL)

The sample shown in the photos is knitted in size L.

FINISHED MEASUREMENTS

Chest: as measured at underarms, 45¾ (46½, 47¼, 48) in / 116 (118, 120, 122) cm

Total Length: 23¼ (23¾, 23¾, 24½) in / 59 (60, 60, 62) cm

MATERIALS

Yarn

CYCA #4 (worsted, afghan, Aran) Hillesvåg Embla (Hifa 3) (100% wool, 230 yd/210 m / 100 g)

Yarn Colors and Amounts:

Peasant Blue 6082: 350 (350, 400, 400) g

Needles: U. S. sizes 6 and 4 (for bands) / 4 and 3.5 mm: 32 in / 80 cm circulars

Notions: 6 buttons of size desired

GAUGE

16 sts and 19 rnds in brioche pattern on larger needles = 4 x 4 in / 10 x 10 cm.

Adjust needle size to obtain correct gauge if necessary.

DOGGER BANK
Brioche-knit vest

BODY

With larger circular, CO 170 (174, 174, 178) sts. Work back and forth in k1, p1 ribbing for 10 rows. Change to brioche:

Row 1: ⋆K1, yo, sl 1 purlwise, k1⋆; rep ⋆ to ⋆ across.

Row 2: ⋆K1 tog with yarnover, yo, sl 1 purlwise, k1⋆; rep ⋆ to ⋆ across.

Rep Row 2 on both sides.

Continue in brioche until body measures 13½ (13¾ 13¾, 14½) in / 34 (35, 35, 37) cm to underarms. Divide body into back—86(88, 88,90) sts—and 2 fronts—42(43, 43, 44) sts each. Pm at each side of piece.

Back: BO 6 sts at each side for underarms and then BO 2 sts 1 time, 1 st 2 times at each side = 70 (72, 72, 74) sts rem. Continue in brioche until body measures 23¾ in / 60 cm or desired length. Place sts on a holder while you knit the fronts.

Front: Work each front separately. At armhole edge, BO 6 sts and then BO 2 sts 1 time, 1 st 2 times. Work 2 more rows and then shape neck: slip first st over next st (as for regular bind-off) at beginning of every neck edge row until 20 sts rem for all sizes. Continue until piece measures 23¼ (23¾, 23¾, 24½) in / 59 (60, 60, 62) cm. Place sts on a holder. Work other front the same way, reversing shaping to correspond.

Join shoulders with mattress or Kitchener st.

ARMHOLE BANDS

With smaller circular, pick up and knit approx. 100 sts around armhole (or fewer for a tighter band if you prefer; in either case, a multiple of 2).

Rnd 1: Work around in k1tbl, p1 ribbing (to avoid holes).

Rnds 2-8: Work around in k1, p1 ribbing.

BO firmly in ribbing. Work opposite armhole band the same way.

NECKBAND

With smaller circular, pick up and knit approx. 120 sts around neckline (30 sts on back and 45 sts on each front). Work front band as for armhole bands, but back and forth over a multiple of 2 + 1 sts.

FRONT BANDS

With smaller circular, pick up and knit 71 sts along front edge, including neckband. Work ribbing back and forth as for armhole and neck bands, but make buttonholes as follows: Begin on RS and work 2 rows. On Row 3, on RS: Work 2 sts, yo, join 2 tog, ⋆work 11 sts, yo, join 2tog⋆; rep ⋆ to ⋆ 5 times and work in ribbing to end of row; turn. Continue in ribbing, working yarnovers in pattern. Work 2 more rows. BO firmly in knitwise so you will have a chain edge.

Weave in all ends neatly on WS.

Sew on buttons. Our version used hand-molded brass buttons from the Sunnmøre Museum.

RØST BANK

V-neck vest

RØST BANK
V-neck vest

SKILL LEVEL

Intermediate

SIZES

S (M, L, XL)

The sample shown in the photos is knitted in size M.

FINISHED MEASUREMENTS

Chest: as measured at underarms, 43¼ (44, 45, 45¾) in / 110 (112, 114, 116) cm

Total Length: 21 (21¼, 21¾, 22) in / 53 (54, 55, 56) cm

MATERIALS

Yarn:

CYCA #3 (DK, light worsted) Sandnes Merinoull (100% Merino wool, 114 yd/104 m / 50 g)

Yarn Colors and Amounts:

Blue-Gray 6071: 350 (350, 400, 400) g

Needles: U. S. size 4 / 3.5 mm: 32 in / 80 cm circular

GAUGE

18 sts and 25 rnds in stockinette = 4 x 4 in / 10 x 10 cm. Adjust needle size to obtain correct gauge if necessary.

BODY

CO 208 (212, 216, 220) sts. Join, being careful not to twist cast-on row; pm for beginning of rnd. Work around in k1, p1 ribbing for 2 in / 5 cm. Knit in stockinette until body is 13½ (13¾, 14¼, 14½) in / 34 (35, 36, 37) cm long or desired length to underarms. BO 6 sts centered at each side = 196 (200, 204, 208) sts rem. Divide work in two = 98 (100, 102, 104) sts each for front and back.

Back: Work back and forth. At each side, BO 2 sts 3 times, and 1 st 5 times. Continue in stockinette until back measures 21 (21¼, 21¾, 22) in / 53 (54, 55, 56) cm. Place sts on a holder.

Front: Work back and forth. Shape armholes and V-neck *at the same time.* Work each side of front separately.

Armhole Shaping: BO 2 sts 4 times, and 1 st 5 times.

V-neck: Decrease 1 st at neck edge on every other row 14 times.

Continue in stockinette until front measures 21 (21¼, 21¾, 22) in / 53 (54, 55, 56) cm. Place sts on a holder.

Work opposite side the same way, reversing shaping to correspond.

Join shoulders with mattress or Kitchener st.

ARMHOLE BANDS

Pick up and knit 76 sts around armhole and work around in k1, p1 ribbing for 1¼ in / 3 cm. BO firmly in ribbing. Work second band the same way.

NECKBAND

Pick up and knit 114 sts around armhole and work around in k1, p1 ribbing for 1¼ in / 3 cm (8 rnds), but at base of V-neck, always knit the 2 center sts. Decrease 1 st on each side of this pair of knit sts on every rnd. BO in ribbing.

Weave in all ends neatly on WS.

FLADEN

Red hat

SKILL LEVEL
Easy to Intermediate

SIZES
One size

FINISHED MEASUREMENTS
Circumference: 22 in / 56 cm
Total Length: 12¾ in / 32 cm (including brim)

MATERIALS
Yarn:
CYCA #2 (sport, baby) Rauma Finull PT2 (100% Norwegian wool, 191 yd/175 m / 50 g)
Yarn Colors and Amounts:
Red 0435: 100 g
Needles: U. S. size 2.5 / 3 mm: 24 in / 60 cm circular and set of 5 dpn

GAUGE
22 sts and 28 rnds in stockinette = 4 x 4 in / 10 x 10 cm
Adjust needle size to obtain correct gauge if necessary.

The hat is worked with a fold-up brim. Once the rim is sewn down, loops are added.

With circular, CO 120 sts. Join, being careful not to twist cast-on row; pm for beginning of rnd. Knit around for 6¼ in / 16 cm.

The hat is now shaped with decreases at each side (e.g., front and back). Pm to make decreasing easier, with markers placed in a system—for example, outside the sts to be knitted together. Decrease as follows: K3, k2tog, k50, k2tog, k6, k2tog, k50, k2tog, k3 = 116 sts rem.

NOTE: When sts no longer fit around circular, change to dpn.

When hat is 7 in / 18 cm long, decrease as follows: K2, k2tog, k50, k2tog, k4, k2tog, k50, k2tog, k2 = 112 sts rem.

When hat is 8 in / 20 cm long, decrease as follows: K1, k2tog, k50, k2tog, k2, k2tog, k50, k2tog, k1 = 108 sts rem.

Continue knitting around until hat is 9 in / 23 cm long. Arrange sts on 4 dpn (= 27 sts on each needle).

Top Shaping:

Dpn 1 and 3: K1 k2tog, knit to end of needle.

Dpn 2 and 4: Knit until 3 sts rem, k2tog, k1.

Knit 7 rnds without decreasing.

Decrease on next rnd.

Knit 6 rnds without decreasing.

Decrease as above on next rnd.

Continue with 1 less rnd between decrease rnds and then decrease on every rnd until 8 sts rem. Cut yarn and draw end through rem sts; tighten. Weave in ends neatly on WS.

TASSEL

Wrap doubled yarn around a piece of cardboard about 2½ in / 6 cm long. The tassel should be loose; wrap about 30 times = 60 strands in tassel. Firmly wrap lower edge of tassel a few times. Cut (leaving long end) and fasten off yarn. Use yarn end to sew tassel securely to top of hat.

LOOP EDGE

Fold in brim, leaving 1½ in / 4 cm on outside; sew down brim. Make loops with doubled yarn and sew 10-11 loops around a pencil or large knitting needle. Do not insert needle through hat. Sew only on the folded-up brim. Sew loops over 2 sts in width. When you need to add yarn, attach ends under the loops.

BLACK VERSION

This hat is shorter than the original; the shaping begins ¾ in / 2 cm sooner.

When hat measures 5½ in / 14 cm, begin decreasing as for red hat and then decrease when hat is 6¼, 7, 8 in / 16, 18, 20 cm long. Knit until hat is 8¼ in / 21 cm long and shape top as for red hat.

Make the loops in two colors, black and mustard.

The red hat is characteristically Norwegian in color and shape, not least with the elaborate loop edging around the folded brim. It was easy to be inspired by classic fishermen's hats. It was also tempting to play a little with the loop edging, and at the same time, knit the hat in black with a less sensational color.

NEWFOUNDLAND BANKS

Long stockings with pointed toe shaping

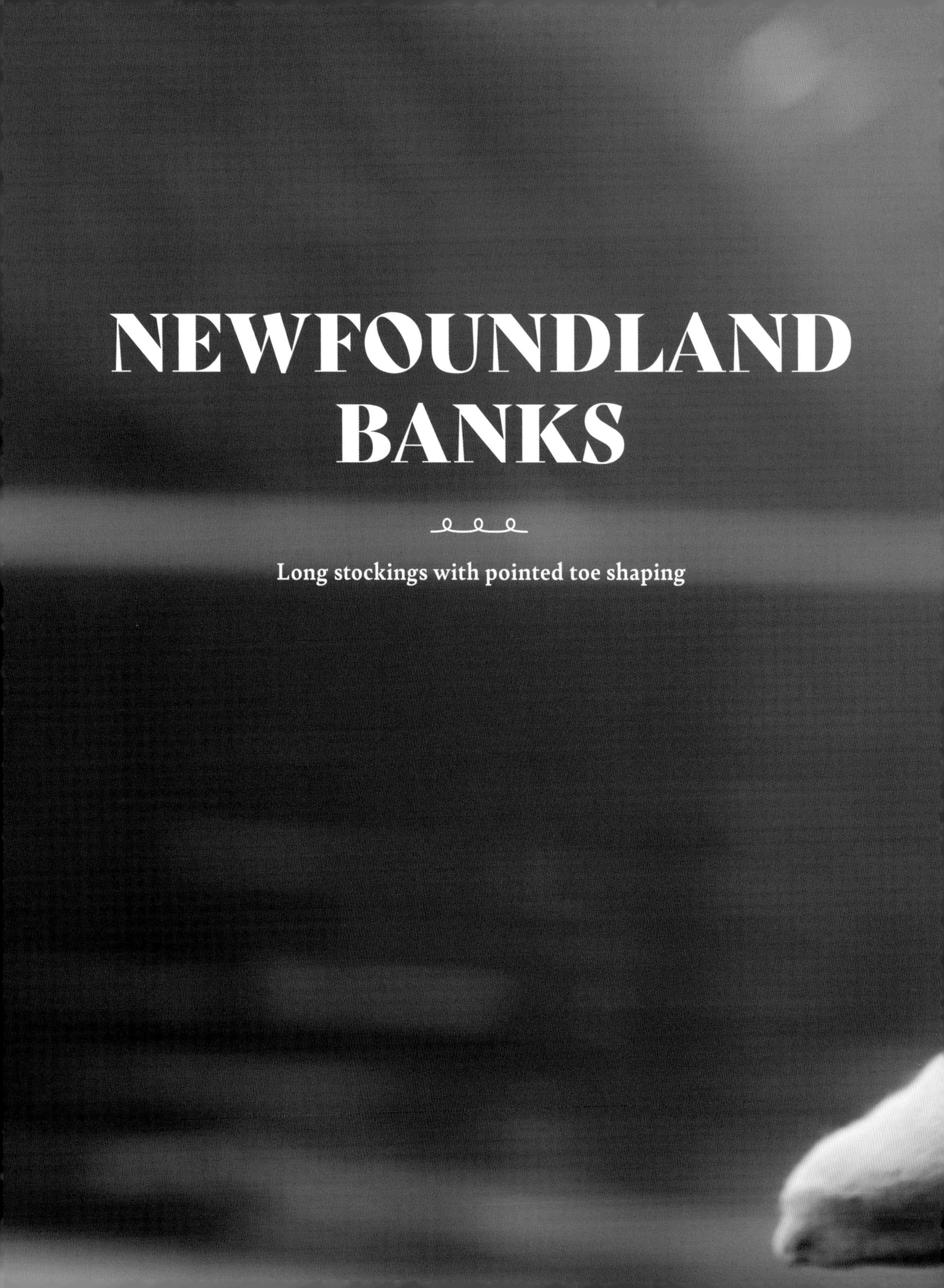

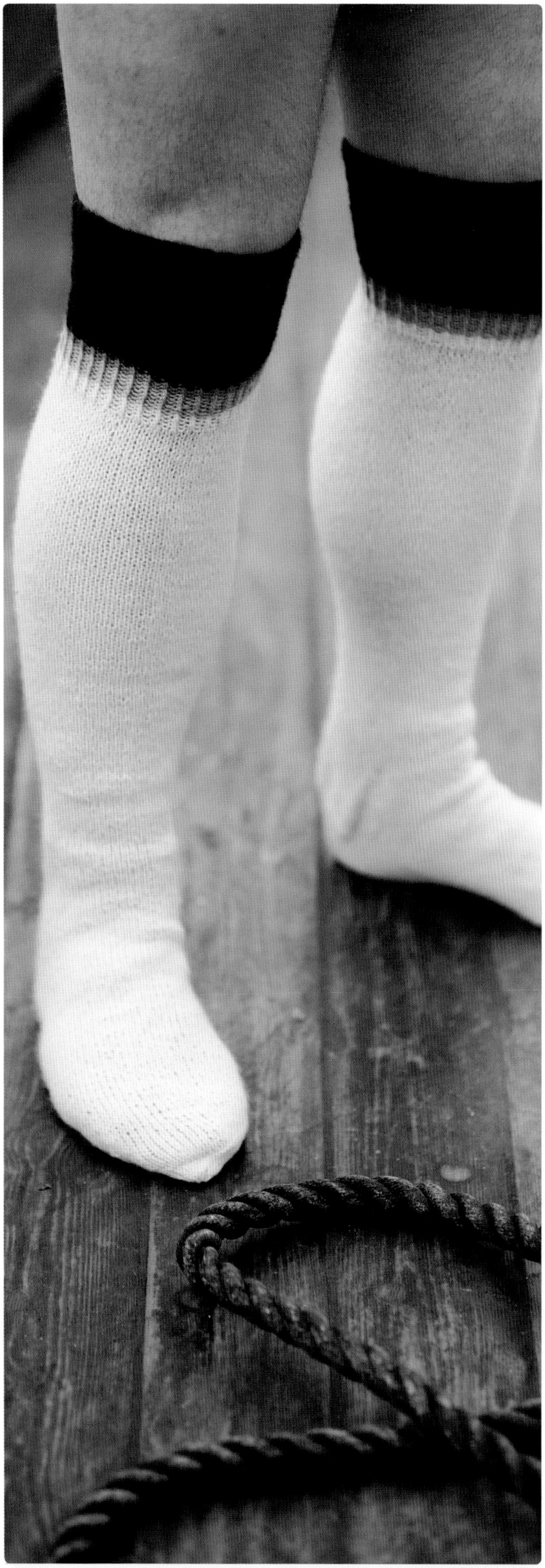

SKILL LEVEL
Intermediate

SIZES
Women's (Men's)
The sample shown in the photos is knitted in the women's size.

FINISHED MEASUREMENTS
Total Length: of foot, 8¾ (11¾) in / 22 (30) cm
Circumference: around ankle, 5¼ (6) in / 13 (15) cm

MATERIALS
Yarn:
CYCA #3 (DK, light worsted) Rauma 3-ply Strikkegarn (100% Norwegian wool, 118 yd/108 m / 50 g)
Yarn Colors and Amounts:
White 101: 200 (200) g
Blue-Black 1387: 50 (50) g
Light Blue 155: 50 (50) g
Orange 161: 50 (50) g
Needles: U. S. size 2.5 / 3 mm: set of 5 dpn

GAUGE
20 sts and 32 rnds in stockinette = 4 x 4 in / 10 x 10 cm.
Adjust needle size to obtain correct gauge if necessary.

With Blue-Black, CO 72 (80) sts. Divide sts onto dpn and join; pm for beginning of rnd. Work around in k1tbl, p1 ribbing for 6¼ in / 16 cm with stripes worked as desired—the example shown has 4 in / 10 cm in Blue-Black, 2 rnds Orange, 6 rnds Light Blue, and 4 rnds White.. Change to stockinette and White when ribbing and stripes are complete, increasing 10 sts evenly spaced around = 86 (94) sts. Knit around until stocking is 3½ (4¼) in / 9 (11) cm long, and then begin shaping. Pm on center back st. Decrease on each side of center back st on every 4th rnd 11 times and then on every 8th rnd 1 (3) times = 58 (62) sts rem. Knit without further shaping until stocking is 21 (23¼) in / 53 (59) cm long or desired length. Now shape heel.

HEEL

Begin with heel flap with 29 (31) sts—14/15 (15/16) sts on sides of center back. Work flap back and forth in stockinette. Sl 1 at beginning of every row for a chain edge. Work 18 (20) rows or to desired length.

Heel Turn: Begin on WS. Use the marker at center back of leg when you decrease as this marks the center back stitch.

Purl until 2 sts past center p2tog, k1; turn.

Knit until 2 sts past center st, sl 1, k1, psso, k1; turn.

Purl to st before gap. P2tog with sts before/after gap, p1.

Knit to st before gap. K2tog with before/after gap, k1.

Rep the last two rows until all the sts across have been worked = 17 sts rem on flap.

Gusset: Pick up and knit 11 (12) sts along each side of flap, knitting across instep in between.

Continue in the round and, on every 4th rnd, decrease with the 2 sts before (k2tog) and after (k2tog tbl) instep until 54 (60) sts rem. Knit around until foot measures 8 (8¾) in / 20 (22) cm or desired length to toe.

TOE

Decrease on each side of foot on every rnd until 8 sts rem. Cut yarn and draw end through rem sts; tighten.

Weave in all ends neatly on WS.

JYSKE REEF

Short stockings with folded cuff and round toe shaping

SKILL LEVEL

Intermediate

SIZES

Women's (Men's)

The sample shown in the photos is knitted in the women's size.

FINISHED MEASUREMENTS

Total Length: of foot, 8¾ (11¾) in / 22 (30) cm

Circumference: around ankle, 5¼ (6) in / 13 (15) cm

MATERIALS

Yarn:

CYCA #3 (DK, light worsted) Rauma 3-ply Strikkegarn (100% Norwegian wool, 118 yd/108 m / 50 g)

Yarn Colors and Amounts:

Blue-Black 1387: 100 (100) g

Blue 167: 50 (50) g

White 101: 50 (50) g

Light Blue 155: 50 (50) g

Needles: U. S. size 4 / 3.5 mm: set of 5 dpn

GAUGE

22 sts and 25 rnds in stockinette = 4 x 4 in / 10 x 10 cm.
Adjust needle size to obtain correct gauge if necessary.

JYSKE REEF

Short stockings with folded cuff and round toe shaping

With Blue-Black, CO 60 (70) sts. Divide sts onto dpn and join; pm for beginning of rnd. Work around in k1, p1 ribbing for 4 rnds. Knit 2 rnds Black and then work following charted pattern. End with 2 rnds Black. Now work eyelet rnd: ★K2tog, yo★; rep ★ to ★ around. Knit 3 rnds. On Rnds 4, 6, and 8, decrease 4 sts evenly spaced around = 48 (58) sts rem. Turn so wrong side of pattern faces out. Continue in stockinette with Black until sock measures 7 (8) in / 18 (20) cm or desired length.

HEEL

Begin with heel flap with sts of Ndls 1 and 4, or 30 (both sizes) sts of center back if you are using a circular. Work flap back and forth in stockinette.

Sl 1 at beginning of every row for a chain edge. Work 18 (20) rows or to desired length. End with a RS row.

Heel Turn: Begin on WS. Use the marker at center back of leg when you decrease as this marks the center back stitch.

Purl until 2 sts past center p2tog, k1; turn.

Knit until 2 sts past center st, sl 1, k1, psso, k1; turn.

Purl to st before gap. P2tog with sts before/after gap, p1.

Knit to st before gap. K2tog with before/after gap, k1.

Rep the last two rows until all the sts across have been worked.

Gusset: Pick up and knit 10 (11) sts along each side of flap (k1tbl into each chain along flap), knitting across instep in between.

Continue in the round, and on every 4th rnd decrease the 2 sts before (k2tog) and after (k2tog tbl) on instep until 58 (64) sts rem. Knit around until foot measures 8 (8¾) in / 20 (22) cm or desired length to toe.

TOE

Divide sts evenly onto 4 dpn. Decrease with k2tog at end of each needle on alternate rnds until 12 sts (3 per needle) rem. K2tog around. Cut yarn and draw end through rem sts; tighten.

Weave in all ends neatly on WS.

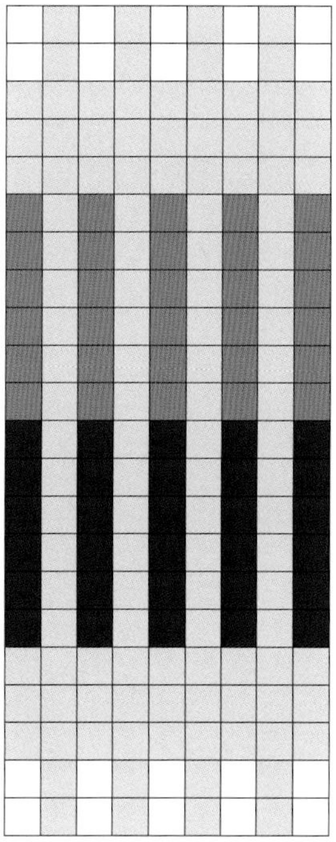

FUGLØY BANK

Scarf

FUGLØY BANK
Scarf

SKILL LEVEL
Easy to Intermediate

SIZES
One size

FINISHED MEASUREMENTS
Width: 8 in / 20 cm
Total Length: 59 in / 150 cm

MATERIALS
Yarn:
CYCA #2 (sport, baby) Hillesvåg Ask—Hifa 2 (100% Norwegian wool, 344 yd/315 m / 100 g)
Yarn Colors and Amounts:
Lime Green 6113: 200 g
Natural White 6057: 50 g
Charcoal Gray 6056: 50 g
Needles: U. S. size 4 / 3.5 mm: 16 in / 40 cm circular

GAUGE
22 sts and 25 rnds in stockinette = 4 x 4 in / 10 x 10 cm. Adjust needle size to obtain correct gauge if necessary.

The scarf is knitted in the round for a double layer.

With Lime Green, CO 81 sts. Knit 1 row and then join to knit in the round; pm for beginning of rnd. Knit 7 rnds in stockinette and then work charted pattern. The first 9 sts are the repeat. After completing pattern rnds, continue Lime Green only and, on the first rnd, decrease 1 st at each side = 79 sts rem. When scarf measures 54¼ in / 138 cm or desired length, increase 1 st at each side. Work charted pattern, but mirror-image so the two panel motifs will point in the same direction. Knit 7 rnds and then end with a garter ridge (purl 1 rnd on RS). BO. Weave in all ends neatly on WS. Seam ends and gently steam press scarf under a damp pressing cloth.

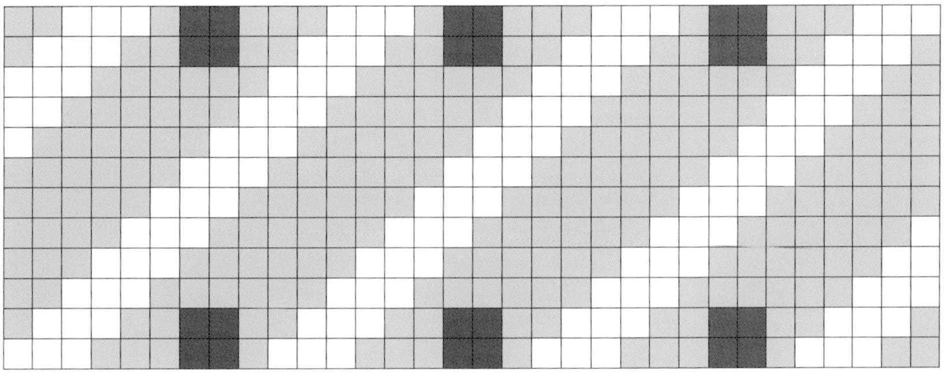

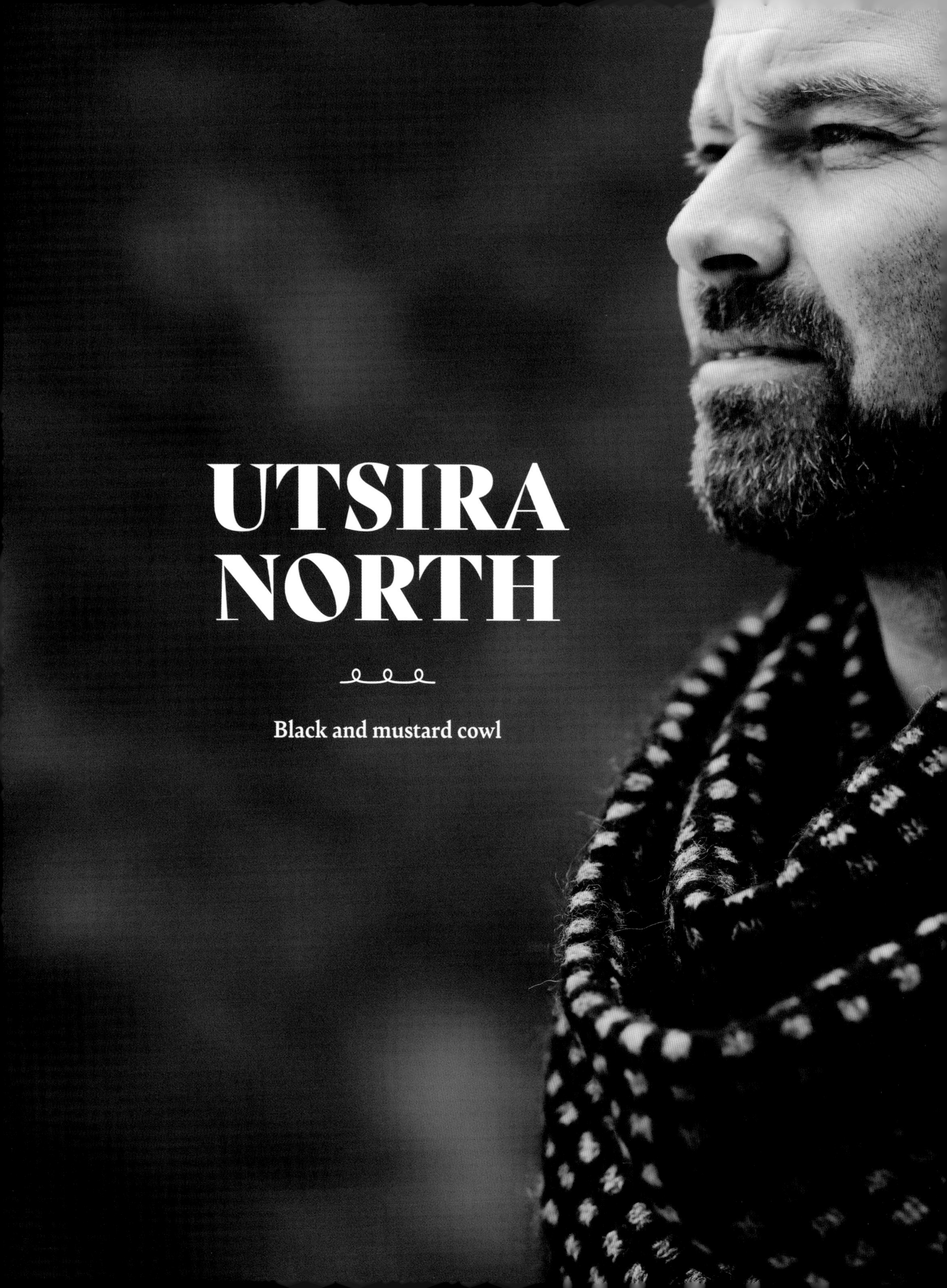

UTSIRA NORTH

Black and mustard cowl

SKILL LEVEL
Intermediate

SIZES
One size

FINISHED MEASUREMENTS
Circumference: 47¼ in / 120 cm

MATERIALS
Yarn:
CYCA #1 (fingering) Hillesvåg Sølje (100% Norwegian pelt wool, 383 yd/350 m / 100 g)
Yarn Colors and Amounts:
Black 2109: 250 g
Yellow 2119: 100 g
Needles: U. S. size 4 / 3.5 mm: 32 in / 80 cm circular

GAUGE
22 sts and 28 rnds in stockinette = 4 x 4 in / 10 x 10 cm.
Adjust needle size to obtain correct gauge if necessary.

The cowl is worked around on a circular and later seamed lengthwise.

With Black, CO 400 sts. Join, being careful not to twist cast-on row; pm for beginning of rnd. Knit 6 rnds in stockinette. Work charted pattern until piece measures 15¾ in / 40 cm. BO. Seam long sides with mattress st.

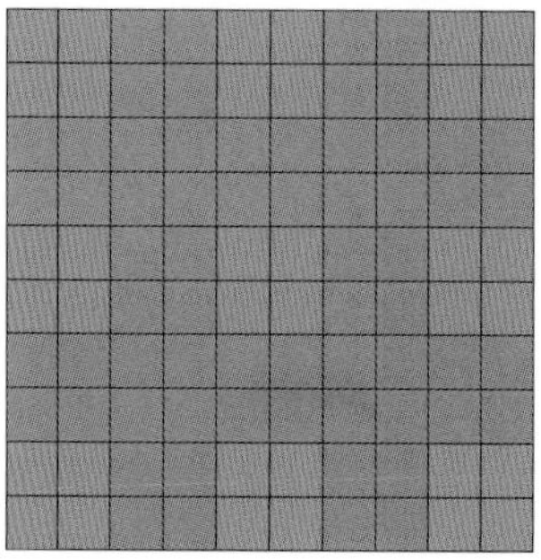

UTSIRA NORTH
Black and mustard cowl

In the painting *A funeral onboard*, by Carl Fredrik Sundt-Hansen (1841-1907), we can see a young man in a blue pullover at the center of the picture. The sweater is a *spunsetrøye*, from the word *spons*, a term for the plug in a fishing boat. The pattern is simple and typical of many Icelanders. We used the motif on a cowl, but it could also be used for many other warm garments that protect against wind and weather.

ORKNEY ISLANDS

Felted mittens

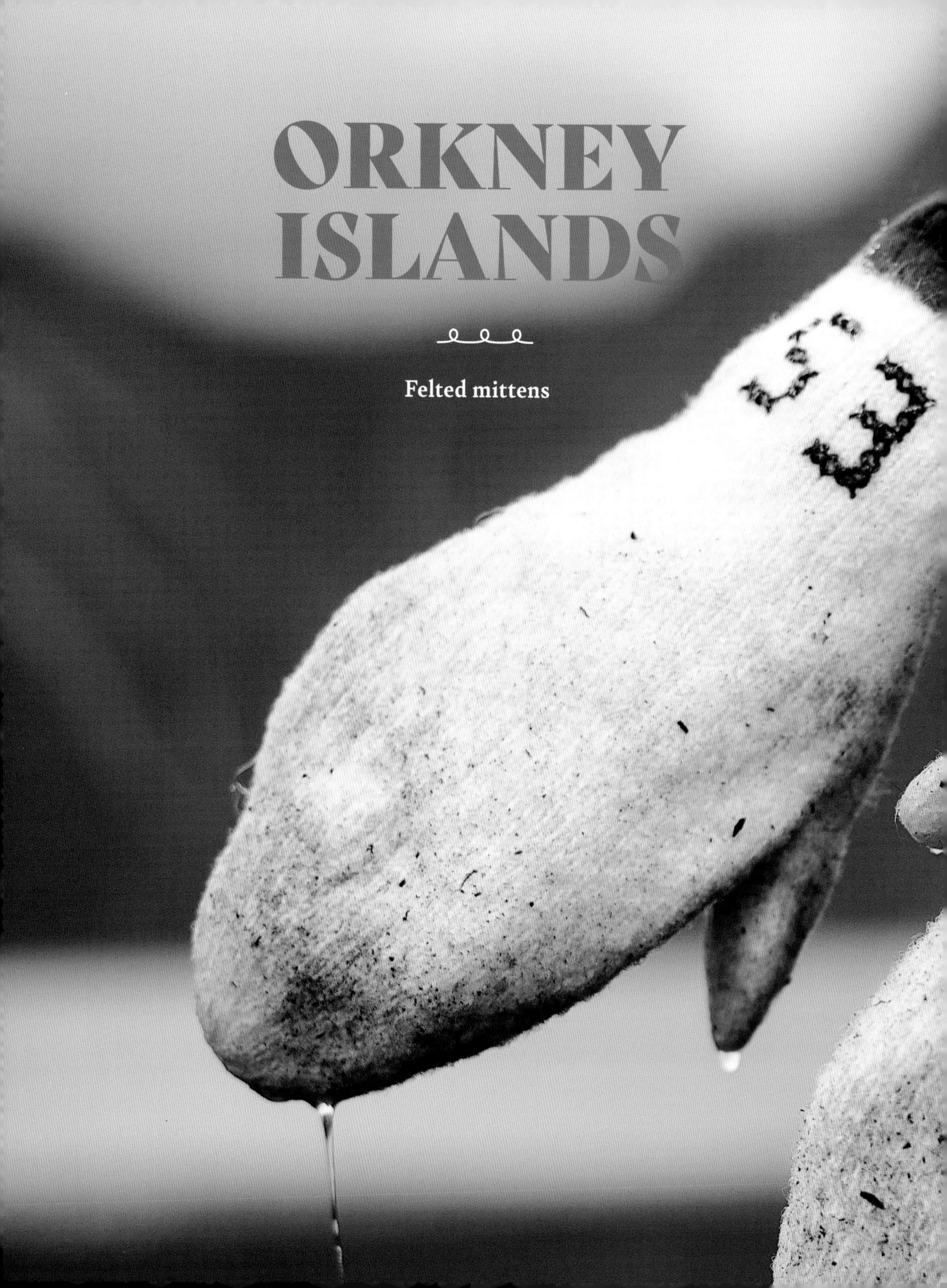

SKILL LEVEL

Easy to Intermediate

SIZES

Women's (Men's)

The sample shown in the photos is knitted in the men's size.

FINISHED MEASUREMENTS

Total Length: approx. 14¼ in / 36 cm (from ribbing to tip of middle finger)

Width: approx. 6 in / 15 cm

MATERIALS

Yarn:

CYCA #3 (DK, light worsted) Rauma 3-ply Strikkegarn (100% Norwegian wool, 118 yd/108 m / 50 g)

Yarn Colors and Amounts:

White 101: 150 g

Blue-Black 1387: 50 g

Dark Red 144: 50 g

Needles: U. S. size 9 / 5.5 mm: set of 5 dpn and short circular

There is no gauge for this project; the degree of felting will determine the final size.

Adjust needle size to obtain correct gauge if necessary.

ORKNEY ISLANDS

Felted mittens

With Black and dpn, CO 46 (52) sts. Divide sts onto 5 dpn and join; pm for beginning of rnd. Work around in k1, p1 ribbing for ¾ in / 2 cm each in Black, Red, and White. Continue in stockinette with White until piece measures 5¼ in / 13 cm. Now begin shaping thumb gusset. Increase 1 st on each side of the first st of rnd. Knit 4 rnds. Increase on each side of the first 3 sts of rnd. Increase the same way on every 5th rnd (with 2 more sts between increases each time) until there are 9 sts in the gusset = 54 (60) sts around. Continue in stockinette until piece measures 8¾ in / 22 cm. Place the 9 thumb gusset sts on a holder. CO 9 (10) new sts over the gap and continue around for 4¼ (5¼) in / 11 (13) cm. Decrease 6 sts evenly spaced around on next rnd and then knit 6 rnds without decreasing. On next rnd, decrease 6 sts evenly spaced around and then knit 5 rnds without decreasing.

Continue shaping as est, decreasing 6 sts evenly divided on a rnd, followed by knit rnds, with 1 less rnd between decrease rnds each time, until 12 (18) sts rem. Knit 1 rnd and then work k2tog around. Cut yarn, draw end through rem sts; tighten.

Thumb: Place the held 9 sts onto dpn, pick up and knit 1 st at each side and in each of the 9 (10) sts cast-on above thumbhole = 20 (21) sts. Knit around until thumb is 2¾ (3¼) in / 7 (8) cm long. Decrease 4 sts evenly spaced around on next rnd and then knit 3 rnds without decreasing. On next rnd, decrease 4 sts evenly spaced around and then knit 2 rnds without decreasing. Decrease 4 sts evenly spaced on next rnd. Cut yarn, draw end through rem sts; tighten.

Make second mitten the same way, but place thumb gusset by increasing 1 st on each side of last st of rnd.

Machine-felt the mittens in 140°F / 60°C water.

After being worn for a time, sea mittens became too small, and too hard to work in, from repeated felting in sea water. Then they were cut up and used as soles for *lugger* which were knitted and sewn *vadmal* shoes worn in heavy snow or in the fishing shanty. But if a sea mitten was still useful and only torn, a new one could be worn inside it. This was where the mitten was exposed to the most wear. Then a new lining was sewn into the mitten.

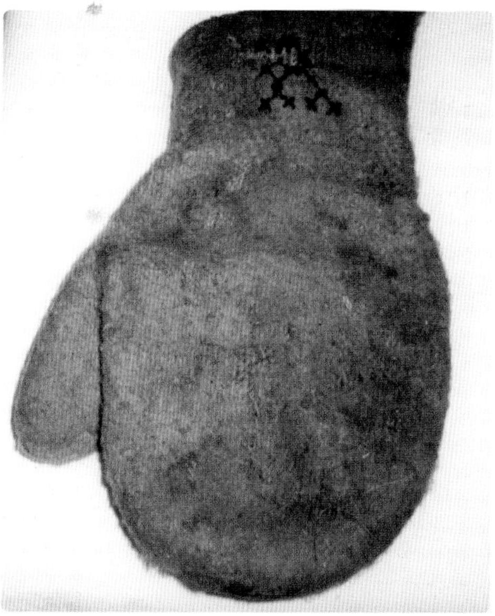

CROSS STITCH ALPHABET

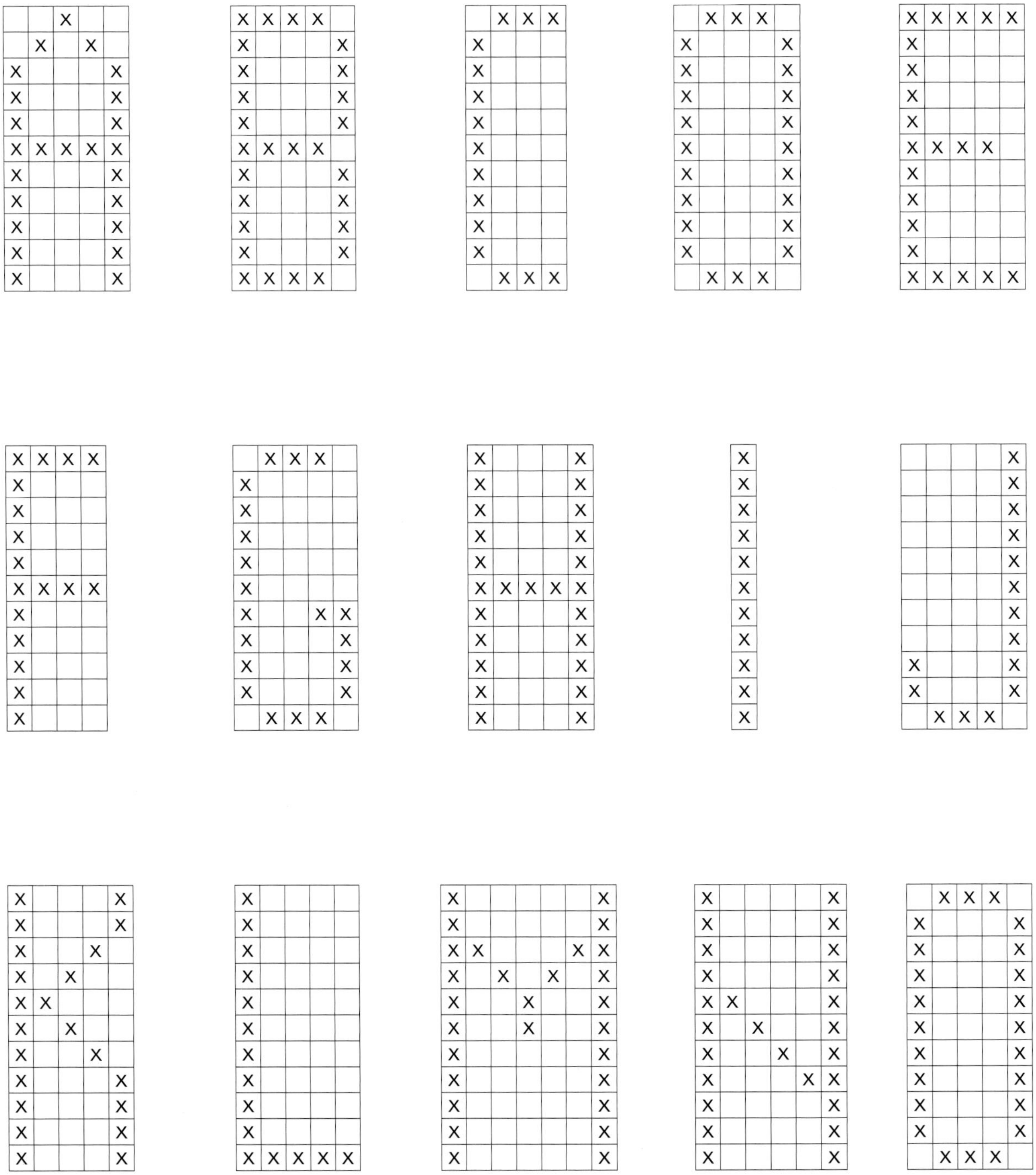

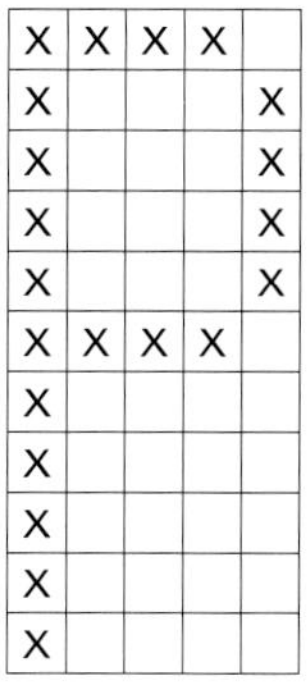
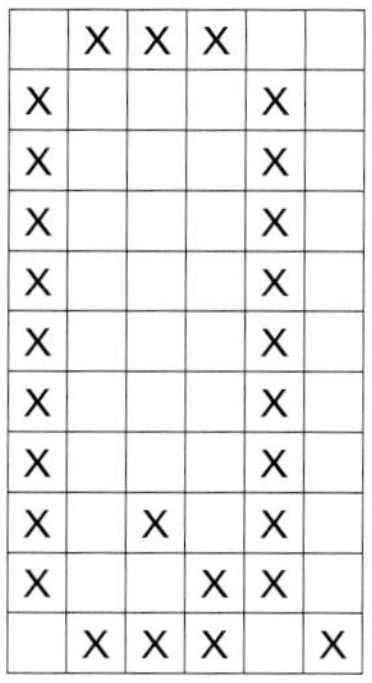
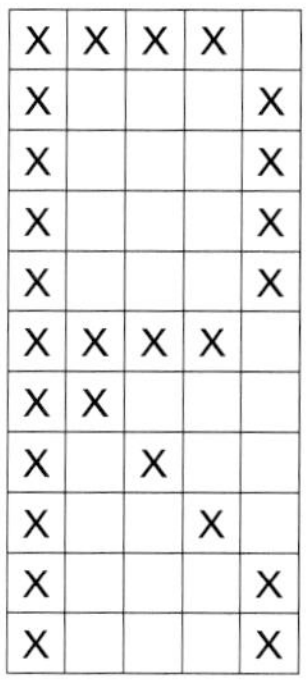
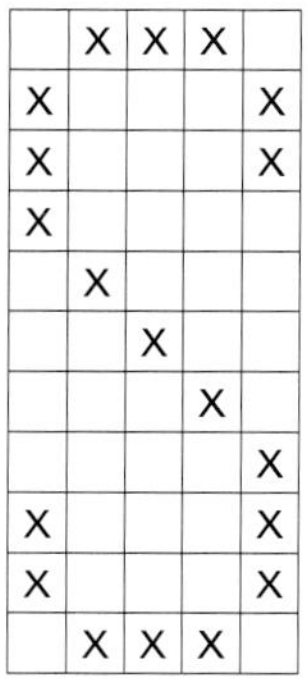
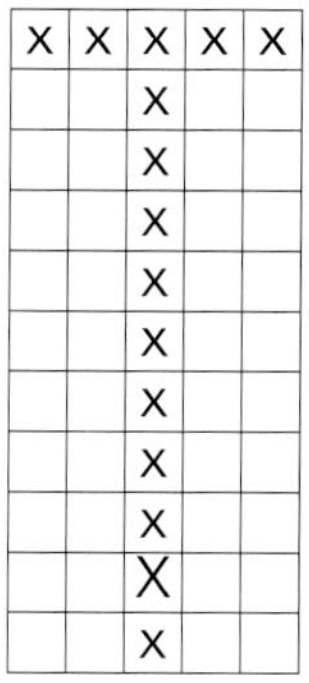
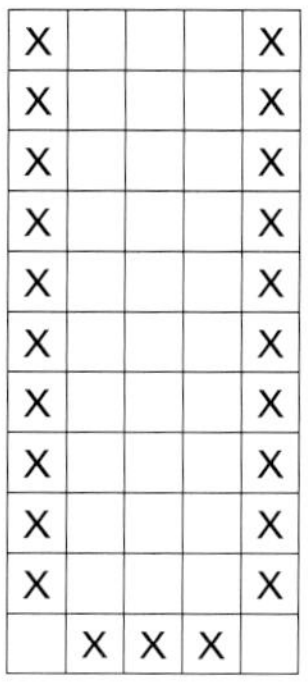
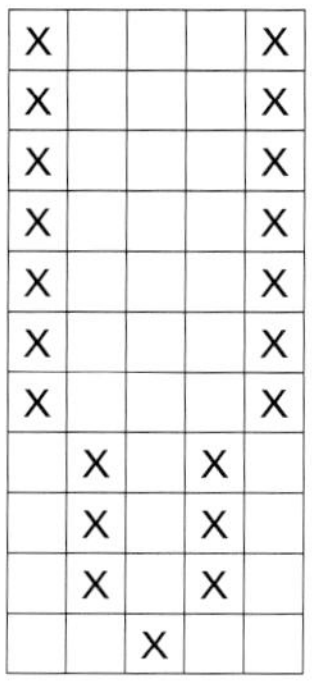
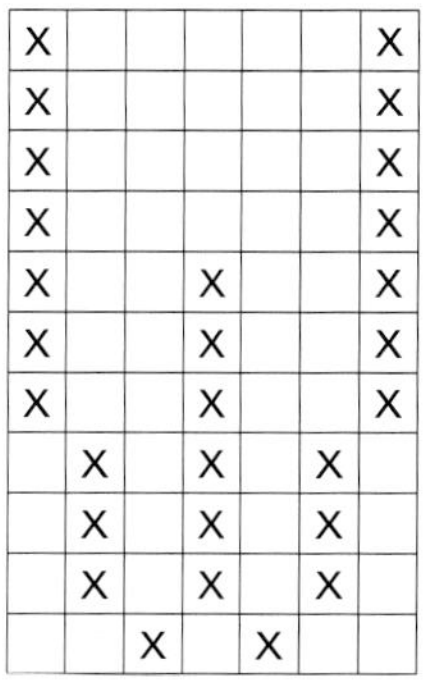
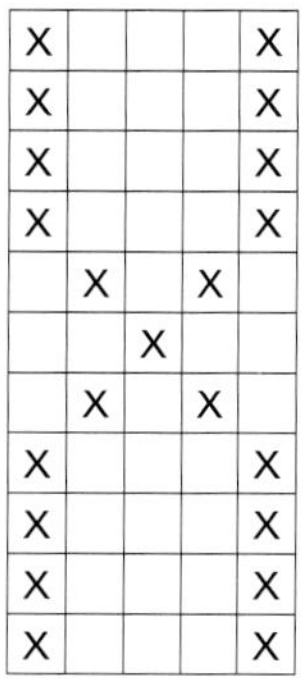
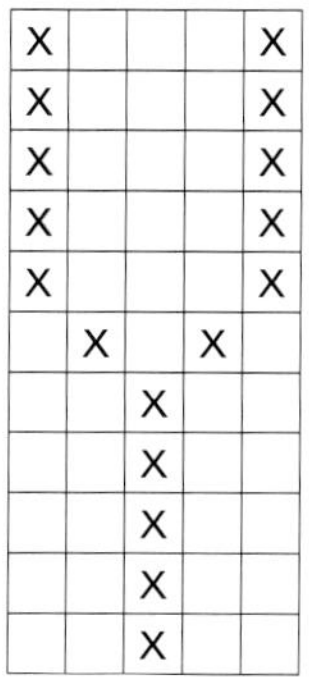
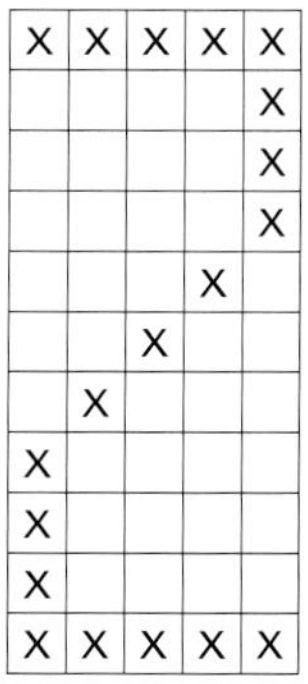
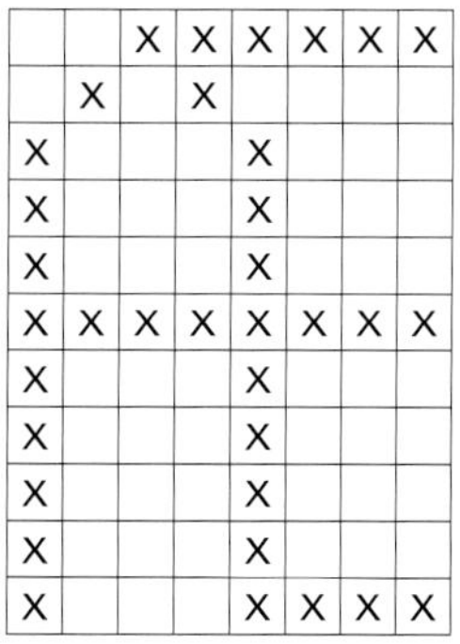
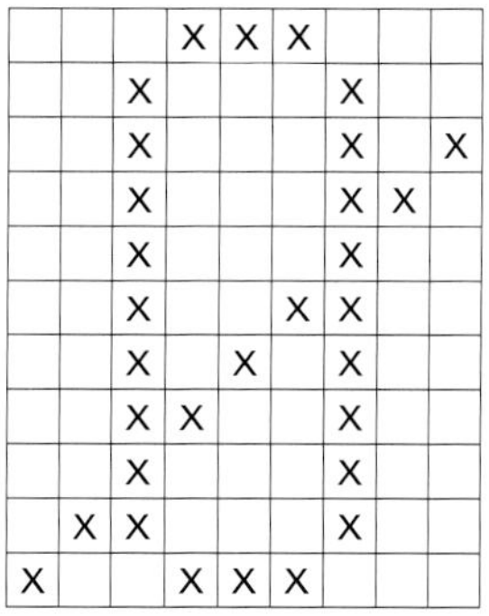
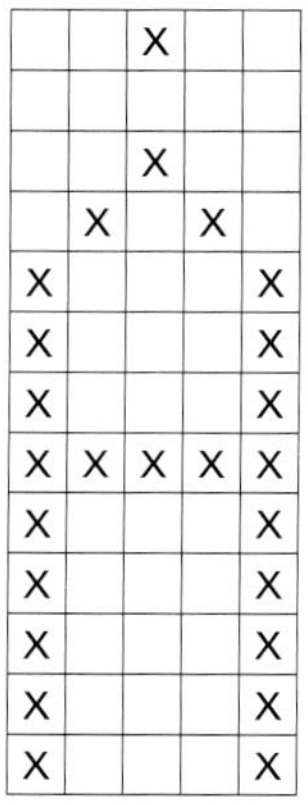

NOTES

1 Grøttland (1978): 130.
2 Trætteberg (1999): 25.
3 Strøm (1762): 399-400.
4 Riksdaler (abbreviated rdl): In Denmark-Norway, riksdaler specie was a silver coin, also called a spesidaler. With the changeover to crowns in 1874, a spesidaler was worth four crowns. Source: *spesidaler—Store norske leksikon* [Big Norwegian Encyclopedia] (snl.no) *riksdaler—Store norske leksikon* (snl.no) [as cited on 4 May 2021].
5 1 mark corresponded to 16 skillings from 1625 to 1813; in 1816, 1 spesidaler was equivalent to 120 skillings, and 1 skilling equaled 3⅓ øre in 1875. Source: *mark—myntenhet—Store norske leksikon* (snl.no), *skilling—Store norske leksikon* (snl.no) [as cited on 4 May 2021].
6 Strøm (1788): 222.
7 Farstad (1991): 9.
8 Farstad (1991): 18 and following.
9 Kjellmo (1996): 83 and following.
10 Grøttland (1978): 130.
11 Official report, 1861-65:5.
12 Official report, 1850-55:17.
13 Sundt (1873): 34.
14 Sundt (1873): 31 and following.
15 Official report, 1851-55:7.
16 Official report, 1856-60-65:1 and following.
17 Trætteberg (1999): 28.
18 Strøm (1788): 223.
19 Trætteberg (1999): 76.
20 A *bismerpund* corresponds to 5.1432 kg or 11.31 pounds. Source: *bismerpund—Store norske leksikon* [Big Norwegian Encyclopedia] (snl.no) [as cited on 16 May 2021].
21 An *anker* was a measure of liquid goods, particularly drinks, as well as for salted herring and fish. In North Norway, it was common for each fisherman to take with them 1 *anker* of buttermilk for the Lofoten cod fishing. In the 1600s, it was calculated that 1 *anker* = 40 *potter*, or approximately 40.8 quarts / 38.6 liters. Source: *Leksikon Anker*—lokalhistoriewiki.no [as cited on 10 April 2021]. *Syre* is sour milk or buttermilk.
22 Dass (1739): 26-27.
23 Heltzen (1834): 246.
24 Heltzen (1834): 246.
25 Trætteberg (1999): 27.
26 *Grener* were rugs used as top and bottom layers for fishermen in the boat and shanty. Wool from the neck, belly, and lower thighs on a Spelsau sheep was considered to be somewhat lower quality than other wool, and was used for weaving these rugs.
27 Trætteberg (1999): 32-33.
28 A *pusseronk* is a cotton work jacket/blouse, sometimes known as a *busserull*.
29 Grøttland (1978): 131 and following.
30 Grøttland (1978): 133.
31 Heltzen (1834):187.
32 Kjellmo (196): 73 and following.
33 Sundt (1869): 237.
34 Kjellmo (196): 90.
35 Kjellmo (196): 23.
36 Trætteberg (1999): 141 and following.
37 Trætteberg (1999): 136.
38 Trætteberg (1999): 143 and following.
39 Trætteberg (1999): 145 and following.
40 Source: *andreakors* (St. Andrew's cross)—*Store norske leksikon* [Big Norwegian Encyclopedia] (snl.no), *åttbladrose* [eight-petal rose])—*Store norske leksikon* (snl.no), *firkant* [square/block]—religion—*Store norske leksikon* (snl.no) [as cited on 4 June 2021].
41 Trætteberg (1999): 146 and following.
42 Trætteberg (1999): 147 and following.
43 Trætteberg (1999): 148.
44 Trætteberg (1999): 160 and following.
45 Trætteberg (1999): 142 and following and 161.
46 Trætteberg (1999): 163 and following.
47 Trætteberg (1999): 150 and following.
48 Trætteberg (1999): 151.
49 Trætteberg (1999): 152 and following.
50 Packet or aniline dyes were chemical dyes discovered by the English chemist Sir William Perkins in the 1850s. It is estimated that aniline dyed yarn came to be sold in Norway by the 1870s. These chemical colors were much brighter than plant dyes and natural sheep colors, and were popular into the twentieth century.
51 Trætteberg (1999): 87 and following.
52 Trætteberg (1999): 90.
53 Trætteberg (1999): 132.
54 Trætteberg (1999): 137.
55 Trætteberg (1999): 60 and following.
56 Gutting includes removing a larger or smaller part of the herring gills, pharynx, and intestines (*gan*). *Ganing* [gutting]—*Store norske leksikon* [Big Norwegian Encyclopedia] (snl.no), [as cited on 31 May 2021].
57 Trætteberg (1999): 95.
58 Trætteberg (1999): 124 and following.
59 Source: *hosebånd* [stocking bands]—*Store norske leksikon* [Big Norwegian Encyclopedia] (snl.no), [as cited on 31 May 2021].
60 Trætteberg (1999): 124.
61 Trætteberg (1999): 79-80.

62 Trætteberg (1999): 100 and following.
63 Trætteberg (1999): 35 and following.
64 Kjellmo (1996): 18 and following.
65 Erbele, et al (1995): 8.
66 Official report 1861-65: 9.
67 Døssland (1990): 453.
68 Trætteberg (1999): 19 and 32.
69 Trætteberg (1999): 38 and 46.
70 Trætteberg (1999): 88.
71 Trætteberg (1999): 92.
72 Grøttland (1978): 127 and following.
73 Official report 1856-60: 7.
74 An *alen* corresponded to 24¾ in / 62.75 cm. Source: *Eldre og fremmede lengde* [old and foreign lengths]—*enheter—Store norske leksikon* [Big Norwegian Encyclopedia] (snl.no), [as cited on 29 May 2021].
75 Sundt (1859): no page number.
76 Strøm (1788): 223-224.
77 Trætteberg (1999): 19; Kjellmo (1996): 89.
78 Kjellmo (1996): 64 and following.
79 Dass (1739): 98 and following.
80 Kjellmo (1996): 64 and following.
81 2 marks correspond to approximately 1.1 lb / .5 kg.
82 Official report 1861-65: 5.
83 Kjellmo (1996): 67.
84 Kjellmo (1996): 70.
85 Trætteberg (1999): 163.
86 Strøm (1762): 553.
87 Strøm (1762): 553.
88 Trætteberg (1999): 89.
89 Trætteberg (1999): 28.
90 Source: *vadmel—Store norske leksikon* [Big Norwegian Encyclopedia] (snl.no), [as cited on 5 June 2021].
91 Trætteberg (1999): 145 and following.
92 Sundbø (2003): 24 and following.
93 Strøm (1762): 552.
94 Trætteberg (1999): 152 and following.
95 Trætteberg (1999): 77, 125 and 146.
96 Trætteberg (1999): 16 and following.
97 Trætteberg (1999): 80 and 168 and following.
98 Trætteberg (1999): 187 and following.
99 Trætteberg (1999): 198 and following.
100 Trætteberg (1999): 219 and following.
101 Trætteberg (1999): 83.
102 Trætteberg (1999): 19 and 142.
103 Trætteberg (1999): 84 and following.
104 Trætteberg (1999): 93 and following.
105 Trætteberg (1999): 76.
106 Farstad (1991): 62.
107 https://www.yrkesfisker.no/no/sikker-fisker/arbeidsmiljo-om-bord/temperatur/ [Cited 20 October 2020].

YARN INFORMATION

Rauma yarns are available from:
The Yarn Guys
theyarnguys.com

The Woolly Thistle
thewoollythistle.com

Sandnes yarns may be purchased (with international shipping charges) from:
Scandinavian Knitting Design
scandinavianknittingdesign.com

Some yarns—Hillesvåg yarns in particular—may be difficult to find. A variety of additional and substitute yarns are available from:
Webs—America's Yarn Store
75 Service Center Road
Northampton, MA 01060
800-367-9327
yarn.com

LoveKnitting.com
loveknitting.com/us

If you are unable to obtain any of the yarn used in this book, it can be replaced with a yarn of a similar weight and composition. Please note, however, the finished projects may vary slightly from those shown, depending on the yarn used. Try www.yarnsub.com for suggestions.

For more information on selecting or substituting yarn, contact your local yarn shop or an online store; they are familiar with all types of yarns and would be happy to help you. Additionally, the online knitting community at Ravelry.com has forums where you can post questions about specific yarns. Yarns come and go so quickly these days and there are so many beautiful yarns available.

SOURCES

Amtmannsinnberetninger. *Beretning om Kongeriget Norges Økonomiske Tilstand 1830–1900.*

Dass, Petter. *Nordlands Trompet.* Kiøbenhavn, 1739.

Erbele, Hannelore m.fl. Tekstil. *Materialkunnskap.* Oslo: Yrkeslitteratur as, 1995.

Farstad, Arnold. *Sjur-ottringen.* Ålesund: Tidsskrift for Sunnmøre Historielag, 1991. 67. årgang. Sunnmøre Historielag, Sunnmøre Museum og Aalesunds Museum.

Grøttland, Kristine Lind. *Daglig brød og daglig dont.* Fra nord-norsk husstell og hjemmeliv. Oslo: Universitetsforlaget, 1978.

Heltzen, Iver Ancher. *Ranens Beskrivelse 1834.* Rana museums- og historielag. Værøy, 1981.

Iversen, Line. *Kulturmøte i museal tekstilsamling.* Et innblikk i kvinneliv og -virke på Sunnmøre ca. 1800 til tidlig 1900-tall. Mastergrad i Kulturmøte, Historisk institutt, Høgskulen i Volda, 2014.

Kjellmo, Ellen Kaia. *Båtrya i gammel og ny tid.* Stamsund: Orkana Forlag AS, 1996.

Strøm, Hans (1762). *Physisk og Oekonomisk Beskrivelse over Fogderiet Søndmør, beliggende i Bergens Stift i Norge.* Oslo: Børsums Forlag, 1957.

Strøm, Hans. *Om Torske Vaar-Fiskeriet paa Sundmøer.* Kiøbenhavn: Kongelige Norske Videnskabers Selskabs Skrifter, Andet Bind, 1788.

Sundbø, Annemor. *Everyday Knitting: Treasures from a Ragpile.* Kristiansand, Norway: Torridal Tweed, 2000.

Sundt, Eilert. *Harham.* Et exempel fra fiskeri-distrikterne. Christiania, 1859.

Sundt, Eilert (1869). *Om renligheds-stellet i Norge.* Oslo: Gyldendal Norsk Forlag, 1975.

Sundt, Eilert (1867–1868). *Om Husfliden i Norge – Til Arbeidets Ære og Arbeidsomhedens Pris.* Oslo: Gyldendal Norsk Forlag, 1975.

Sundt, Eilert (1873). *Om Huslivet i Norge. – Fortsættelse af Bogen fra 1869 «Om Renlighedstellet i Norge». Og med særligt hensyn til de tre vestlandske Amter Romsdal samt Nordre og Søndre Bergenhus.* Oslo: Gyldendal Norsk Forlag, 1976.

Trætteberg, Gunvor Ingstad. *Skinnhyre og sjøklær.* Fiskerbondens utrustning på 1700- og 1800-tallet. Landbruksforlaget, 1999.